D1516484

THE BILINGUAL REVOLUTION

THE FUTURE OF EDUCATION IS IN TWO LANGUAGES

Fabrice Jaumont

Foreword by Ofelia Garcia

TBR Books
Brooklyn, New York

TBR Books
146 Norman Avenue
Brooklyn, New York
www.tbr-books.com

For more information, please contact TBR Books at contact@tbr-books.com

Front Cover Illustration © Raymond Verdaguer
Back Cover Photo © Jonas Cuénin
Cover Design © Nathalie Charles

The Bilingual Revolution/ Fabrice Jaumont. – 2nd ed.
ISBN 978-1-9476260-0-3 (paperback)
ISBN 978-1-9476260-3-4 (hardcover)
ISBN 978-1-9476260-2-7 (eBook)
ISBN 978-1-947626-06-5 (audio book)
The Library of Congress has catalogued the TBR Books hardcover edition as follows
Jaumont, Fabrice
  The Bilingual Revolution: The Future of Education is in Two Languages/ Fabrice Jaumont
  Includes bibliographical references and index
  Library of Congress Control Number 2017949229

Praises

"Multilingualism is no longer a luxury afforded only to the affluent or lucky few who can attend dual-language schools; it is a critical 21st century skill that children will need to be successful in their future work and life. Jaumont's Bilingual Revolution in many ways levels the playing field by sharing various world language program models and best practices, while also demystifying language learning so that parents and educators have a feasible roadmap to begin a "revolution" of their own. The Bilingual Revolution is a must read for any parent who wants to ensure their child will be world and workforce ready."

—Angela Jackson, Founder, Global Language Project

"Jaumont's book stands on the edge of the nascent bilingual revolution running through the United States' school system and asks how it might be improved and encouraged. Jaumont describes the country's growing enthusiasm for multilingual education—and provides a roadmap for communities who want to join the movement."

—Conor Williams, PhD
Senior Researcher, New America's Education Policy Program
Founder, DLL National Work Group

"This engaging book tells the story of the history of bilingual education in the U.S.A. and the social forces that shaped that trajectory from a perspective that is both personal and scholarly. The center piece is a 'how to' manual for setting up your own bilingual school and in so doing creating your own revolution. Recommended for parents, teachers, and everyone who thinks that languages are important."

—Ellen Bialystok, OC, PhD, FRSC,
Walter Gordon York Research Chair in Lifespan Cognitive Development,
York University

Also by Fabrice Jaumont

Unequal Partners: American Foundations and Higher Education Development in Africa. New York, NY : Palgrave-MacMillan, 2016.

The Bilingual Revolution: The Future of Education is in Two Languages. New York, NY: TBR Books, 2017. Also available in Arabic, Chinese, French, German, Russian, and Spanish.

Partenaires inégaux. Fondations américaines et universités en Afrique Paris : Éditions de la Maison des sciences de l'homme, collection "Le (bien) commun", 2018.

Stanley Kubrick: The Odysseys. New York, NY: Books We Live By, 2018).

Contents

Preface

The idea for this book came about through my efforts to support the development of language education in American public schools since the late 1990s. I moved to the United States in 1997 to work as an education liaison for the French Consulate in Boston, during which time I had the opportunity to visit numerous schools across the country. My first encounter with immersion schools was in Massachusetts, in the towns of Milton and Holliston. As a native of France, these programs immediately caught my attention because they offered immersive curricula in French, from Kindergarten to high school, to children in the United States who did not necessarily have a particular connection to the French language or a French-speaking country. More importantly, these programs were in public schools, free of charge, and therefore accessible to every student and family. This made a strong impression on me as I witnessed children mastering my own native language, eventually becoming bilingual and biliterate themselves.

Over the years, the French immersion schools in Massachusetts I first visited have educated thousands upon thousands of children through immersion programs. These schools, along with the educators and the parents that stand behind them, continue to inspire me to this day and have had an enormous influence on my own life and career. Soon after visiting them, I became a director at a private international school in Boston where I managed a rigorous bilingual international program. The families that attended the school believed in its curriculum and language-oriented approach. They saw that the program had the potential to provide life-long skills to their children, and could open doors to a myriad of rewarding opportunities. Like myself, they were convinced of the incredible benefits of bilingualism and were determined to give their children the gift of language.

In 2001, I moved to New York City to become an Education Attaché for the Embassy of France, a position which I still hold today. My work includes collaboration with numerous school leaders, teachers, parent groups, and community organizations. Together, we developed an initiative that led to the creation of New York City's first French-English

i

dual-language programs in public schools. In addition to that, I was involved in similar initiatives that led to the creation of dual-language programs in Japanese, German, Italian, and Russian. In 2014, our story caught the attention of numerous media outlets including the New York Times, which published an article on the rise of dual-language programs in New York that highlighted their potential positive impact on public school communities. An interesting debate ensued regarding the relevance of teaching foreign languages today in the United States and the validity of early language acquisition. This debate, and the questions that it raised among parents within several linguistic communities, pushed me to write this book.

As the father of two bilingual and bicultural girls who attend a dual-language program in a public school in Brooklyn, I am also deeply attached to the concept of dual-language education as a way to both sustain a cultural heritage and acquire a second language. I wanted the book to be directed towards parents, with the goal of providing accessible knowledge, guidance, and encouragement as they consider implementing a dual-language program in their community or school. In that spirit, the book provides a roadmap for parents willing to embark on such an initiative, along with suggested steps to follow, examples, and testimonies from parents and educators who have chosen a similar path.

Through my research, as well as my professional and personal experiences, I have found that children who have had a bilingual upbringing enjoy numerous benefits beyond the acquisition of another language, including a better appreciation of other cultures, other individuals, and even oneself. Additionally, I have come to believe that the cognitive, emotional, and social advantages of being bilingual, biliterate, and multicultural should simply not be limited to private schools and those who can afford to attend them. In my opinion, dual-language education is a universal good that ought to be developed everywhere, as it can positively transform a child, a family, a school, a community, and even a country. It is with this belief and with the conviction that parents can make a difference that I share this book in the hope that more bilingual programs will sprout in schools around the world.

Fabrice Jaumont. 21 August 2017. New York, NY.

Acknowledgements

Without the support and encouragement of many individuals and organizations, this book would not have been completed. Appreciation is expressed to those who gave of their time by granting me interviews, by making information available for this study, by sharing with me their knowledge, passion, or expertise on the topics that I discuss in the book, and by keeping the flame of the bilingual revolution alive. For all this and for their assistance and encouragement at various stages, special appreciation is expressed to:

Marty Abbott, Mary Acosta, Maha Afifi, Ria Aichour, Carine Allaf, Debbie Almontaser, Tamara Alsace, Michele Amar, Gabrielle Amar-Ouimet, Anna Cano Amato, Shareen Anderson, Ana Ines Ansaldo, Gérard Araud, Carmen Asselta, Laetitia Atlani-Duault, Laurent Auffret, Milady Baez, Corinne Bal, Lena Barbera-Johnson, Isabelle Barrière, Gretchen Baudenbacher, Antonin Baudry, Celine Beloeil, Franck Benayoun, Alessandra Benedicty, Anne Benoit, Adrienne Berman, Lenore Berner, Vanessa Bertelli, Anne Berthelot, Ellen Bialystok, Bruno Bich, Josée Bienvenu, Edith Boncompain, Piera Bonerba, Habiba Boumlik, Claire Bourgeois, Marie Bouteillon, Iwona Borys, Gilles Bransbourg, Alexis Buisson, Gracie Burke, Therese Caccavale, Talcott Camp, Richard Carranza, Robert Celic, Karyn Chemin, Lanny Cheuck, Joelle Ciesielski, Andrew Clark, Karl Cogard, Elisa Conigliaro, Ilaria Costa, Earlene Cruz, Jonas Cuénin, Elizabeth Czastkiewizc, Elizabeth Rose Daly, Caroline Daoud, Bénédicte de Montlaur, Virgil de Voldère, Merilla Deeb, Jean-Cosme Delaloye, François Delattre, Katie Dello Stritto, Anaïs Digonnet, Carmen Dinos, Verena Dobnik, Karin Dogny, Fabienne Doucet, Jean-Claude Duthion, Louis Duvernois, Joseph Dunn, Jont Enroth, Gérard Epelbaum, Anne-Laure Faillard, Carmen Fariña, André Ferrand, Martina Ferrari, Yuli Fisher, Nelson Flores, Tara Fortune, Heather Foster-Mann, Jesus Fraga, Naomi Fraser, Ofelia Garcia, Banafche Garnier, Muriel Gassan, Giselle Gault-McGee, Hélène Godec, Kevin Goetz, Enrique Gonzalez, Vartan Gregorian, Francois Grosjean, Tommi Grover, Anne-Sophie Gueguen, Bruce Hale, Skip Hale, Phillip Hall, Terri Hammat, Vanessa Handal, Mary Ann Hansen, Robert Hansen, Alan and Catherine

Harper, Elisabeth Hayes, Carol Heeraman, Gaby Hegan, Hannah Helms, Christine Hélot, Annie Heminway, Juliette Hirsch, Vanessa Hradsky, Peep Hughes, Sandrine Humbert, Marion Hurstel, Sandrine Isambert, Olga Ilyashenko, Angelica Infante, Angela Jackson, Maria Jaya, Jillian Juman, Olga Kagan, Hee Jin Kan, Soumountha Keophilavong, Celine Keshishian, Jack Klempay, Tatyana Kleyn, Maria Kot, Jennifer Kozel, Thierry Roland Kranzer, Thomas Kwai, Nari Kye, Anne Lair, Mathilde Landier, Sophie Larruchon, David Lasserre, Annie Le, Benoit Le Devedec, Virginie Le Lan, Alessia Lefebure, Annique Leman, Irene Leon, Olga Liamkina, Diana Limongi,, Evelyn Lolis, Susan Long, Marcello Lucchetta, Sean Lynch, Chantal Manès, Laurent Marchand, Gaétan Mathieu, Marc Maurice, Jennifer Mazigh, Hélène Maubourguet, Mimi Met, Thomas Michelon, Yumi Miki, Jeffrey Miller, Jean Mirvil, Belinda Mondjo, Christophe Monier, Oisín Muldowney, Monica Muller, Kaye Murdock, Tomoko Nakano, Florence Nash, Martina Nerrant, Naomi Nocera, Sophie Norton, Sandie Noyola, Toby Oppenheimer, Bahar Otcu-Grillman, David Ouimet, Nilda Pabon, Daniel and Ailene Palombo, Lucia Pasqualini, Marie Patou, Guénola Pellen, Danielle Pergament, Jayme Perlman, Catherine Pétillon, Joy Peyton, Andrea Pfeil, Magali Philip, Catherine Poisson, Kim Potowski, Florence Poussin, Stefania Puxeddu, Dana Raciunas, Blake Ramsey, Olivia Jones Ramsey, Jeannie Rennie, Luis Reyes, Nancy Rhodes, Pascale Richard, Zachary Richard, Kareen Rispal, William Rivers, Joseph Rizzi, Gregg Roberts, Ana Roca, Nicky Kram Rosen, Rita Rosenback, Linda Rosenbury, Alfred and Jane Ross, Keith Ryan, Emmanuel Saint-Martin, Maria Santos, Harriet Saxon, Clémence Schulenburg, Julia Schulz, Kirk Semple, Marie-Pierre Serra-Orts, Beth Shair, Tina Simon, Elisa Simonot, Lea Joly Sloan, Olivier Souchard, Jack Spatola, Julia Stoyanovich, Ircania Stylianou, Marcelo Suárez-Orozco, Robin Sundick, Claire Sylvan, Véronique Sweet, Aya Taylor, Mary-Powell Thomas, Christelle Thouvenin, Paul Robert Tiendrébéogo, Annie Vanrenterghem-Raven, Yalitza Vasquez, Raymond Verdaguer, Louise Alfano Verdemare, Nancy Villarreal de Adler, Pierre Vimont, Cécile Walschaerts, Shimon Waronker, Katrine Watkins, Sylvia Wellhöfer, Katja Wiesbrock-Donovan, Conor Williams, Alicja Winnicki, Ron Woo, Li Yan, Mika Yokobori, Brian Zager, Zeena Zakharia, Donna Zilkha, and Amy Zimmer.

Finally, I want to thank Margaret Liston for her incredible talent and perseverance while editing my numerous drafts, and Darcey Hale, my 83-year-old "American mother" whose meticulous, word-by-word, line-by-line examination of my text has brought it extra clarity and concision. Gratitude also goes to my wife, Nathalie, and my daughters, Cléa and Félicie, for bringing me the encouragements and strength to complete this project.

Bilingual Education:
Making a U-Turn with Parents and
Communities

By Ofelia García

This book makes a most important contribution because it focuses on a topic that is often absent—that of the important role that *parents* of different ethnolinguistic backgrounds have in shaping an appropriate education for their children in the United States. Usually books on bilingual education are for teachers and little attention has been previously paid to how families can act to ensure that American public schools develop bilingual education programs for their children. The most important story told by Fabrice Jaumont in this book is that of the *desire of American families* to have their children schooled bilingually, in English, but also in a language that has deep connections to them. Contrary to popular opinion, American families with different ethnolinguistic backgrounds are interested in developing bilingual education programs for their children.

Whereas the federal government and state education departments have viewed the use of languages other than English in educating American children with suspicion, middle-class American families today are involved in what Fabrice Jaumont calls a revolution, a revolution led from the bottom up, by families who appreciate the value of bilingualism because it is part of their American identity. And this is the value of Jaumont's book —it reminds us that *bilingual education is an American tradition*, a tradition, however, that has always been mired in tensions, controversy and struggle, as I show below.

Fabrice Jaumont's book recaptures the promise of a bilingual education tradition and reminds us that *all Americans*—those with different racial identities, social class, and immigration history—have different linguistic and cultural practices. In this book, American parents whose children's heritages include linguistic practices that have traces of what are considered Arabic, Chinese, English, French, Japanese, Italian, German, Polish, Russian, and Spanish, understand these practices to be important. For these parents, a bilingual education is important not because of any connection to the past or foreign lands, but to recognize an American multilingual present and forge the possibilities of a more inclusive future for all American children.

Here I trace both the tradition of American bilingual education, as well as the opposition to it. By also analyzing the ways in which bilingual education was reinterpreted in the second half of the 20th century, I describe how Jaumont's book proposes *a U-turn for bilingual education*, a return to its beginnings. Rather than starting with government mandates and regulations and focusing only on those who lack—lack English, lack years of residency, lack economic means—Jaumont proposes that we start with the wishes of ethnolinguistic communities (old and new) to bilingually educate their children. The bilingual education programs that Jaumont portrays in this book *start with the children and the desires of parents and communities* for their education. But this is not an easy feat. The road is long, with many a winding turn, for we would have to change the English-only path that has been taken by American public schools. The most important aspect of Jaumont's book is then the roadmap that he gives families, a roadmap that can help them shape the path as they make a new road upon walking, as they make, as Antonio Machado, the Spanish poet, says, "camino al andar."

A Tradition of American Bilingual Education and Opposition

Throughout the 18th century, the German-speaking communities in Pennsylvania and Ohio established schools where German was used as the medium of education (Crawford, 2004; García, 2009). These schools grew throughout the 19th century and increasingly became more like the bilingual programs we know today. For example, during the second half of the 19th century, children in Cincinnati split their school week between an

English and a German teacher. In 1837, a year before the first all-English public school opened in St. Louis, a German-English public school was established. In the bilingual public schools of St. Louis, one-fourth of the students during the second half of the 19th century were not of German descent, reminiscent of the present trend of what we call today "two-way dual-language," a type of bilingual education where students of ethnolinguistic minorities and English-speaking majorities are educated jointly to develop the bilingualism of all. And yet, by the late 19th century, St. Louis terminated its bilingual education policy, restricting the teaching of German to public secondary schools.

The opposition to a U.S. tradition of bilingual education is also not new. From its beginnings, those considered non-whites—Native Americans and enslaved Africans—were not given any voice; their language practices were silenced as they were annihilated and excluded from education. The Treaty of Guadalupe Hidalgo (1848), which ended the Mexican-American war, made Spanish visible in what were then U.S. territories (which encompass today California, Arizona, Texas, Nevada, New Mexico, Utah, and parts of Colorado and Wyoming). In 1874, in what became the territory of New Mexico (which included present-day Arizona and New Mexico), only five percent of schools were in English only. Fifteen years later, in 1889, that percentage had increased to forty-two percent (del Valle, 2003). English-only schooling became the norm in schools in New Mexico by the end of the 19th century. When California became a state in 1850, it was decreed that schools would be in English and Spanish. However, five years later, English was declared the only language of instruction (Castellanos, 1983). The growth of Spanish in U.S. territory had to be stopped. Throughout the 19th century, Americans not considered white were poorly educated (if at all) in segregated English-only schools, the most important instrument in the extinction of languages other than English in the United States.

The opposition to bilingual education and the teaching of the languages of those considered "others" was gradually extended to all ethnolinguistic groups. After the Louisiana Purchase in 1803, schools in Louisiana had provided bilingual instruction in French and English. By 1921 the Louisiana state constitution required that all public schools teach in English only (del Valle, 2003). The very varied linguistic practices of Swedes, Ukrainians, Finns, Lithuanians, Poles, Slovaks, Greeks, Russians, Italians, and Jews became suspect as immigration grew at the turn of the

20th century. President Theodore Roosevelt captured the mood of the time when he said in 1915 that "it would not be merely a misfortune but a crime to perpetuate differences of language in this country" and recommended that immigrants who had not learned English after five years should be returned to their countries (cited in Castellanos, 1983, p. 40). When Germany became the enemy of the United States in the First World War, the German language was also declared suspect. Bilingual education was abandoned, and even the study of languages considered "foreign" was restricted. By 1923, when the U.S. Supreme Court struck down language-restrictive laws in three states in *Meyer v. Nebraska*, there were thirty-four states that forbade the use of languages other than English for instruction (Crawford, 2004; García, 2009).

Public bilingual education for ethnolinguistic communities did not make a quick comeback. When the restriction was lifted, ethnolinguistic groups that had the necessary economic means established complementary schools that offered instruction to support their linguistic and cultural practices and that functioned on weekends or after-school. Some communities were able to develop non-public bilingual schools. For example, Epstein (1977) tells us that by 1940 the Franco-American community had a total of 249 bilingual schools "mi-anglais, mi-français, à part égales" (Epstein, 1977, p. 37). But despite a few successful efforts, language minority groups that had been also racialized in an effort to conquer them and colonize them—Native Americans, Mexican Americans and other Latin@s—did not have the economic means or the political power to establish their own bilingual schools.

The American Bilingual Education Tradition Reinterpreted

Throughout the Civil Rights era, the Latin@ community called for bilingual education, not only as a way of educating their children, but also as a "means to realize the promise of equal citizenship" (Del Valle, 1998, p. 194). This included radical Latin@ political organizations such as the Brown Berets and the Young Lords who saw bilingual education as a way to exert community control and to improve the economy of the Latin@ community (Flores, 2016; Flores & García, forthcoming). But what the Latin@ community got was something completely different.

In 1965, under President Lyndon Johnson's War on Poverty, Congress passed The Elementary and Secondary Education Act (ESEA). And three years later, in 1968, ESEA was reauthorized and amended to include Title VII, The Bilingual Education Act. The legislation provided funds to school districts that established bilingual programs to teach students who did not speak English and were in need of remediation, mostly back then Mexican Americans and Puerto Ricans, but also Native Americans, Native Hawaiians, and Alaskan natives. Bilingual education came back into public schools in a new guise, one that was limited to those considered by the federal government as "Limited English Proficient," and that did not respond to the desires of different ethnolinguistic communities, even the ones that they were supposed to be helping. Eventually, these federally-funded programs came to be defined as transitional, with the language other than English used only to remediate the lack of English, and only transitionally. From the beginning, there was tension between ethnolinguistic communities who insisted that they wanted bilingual education for their children, even though they were already bilingual. The scene was set for what has been a half-century of confusion and continued attacks.

The federal government expected the funds to be used only for transitional bilingual education. But school districts with mostly Latin@ and Native Americans educators and students, but also some with other ethnolinguistic communities, used their bilingual programs to serve families—some whose children were highly bilingual, others who were not. The attacks from many on these developmental maintenance bilingual education programs were vicious. In 1980, President Ronald Reagan, shortly after taking office, summarized what became the popular opinion of the powerful majority:

> [I]t is absolutely wrong and against American concepts to have a bilingual education program that is now openly, admittedly dedicated to preserving their native language and never getting them adequate in English so they can go out into the job market and participate (cited in García, 2009).

Gradually, the tide against bilingual education turned even in states that had previously supported it. Three states — California, Massachusetts and Arizona— declared bilingual education illegal around the turn of the 21st century, and bilingual education programs all across the nation started to close down (Menken & Solorza, 2014). Many bilingual education programs were substituted by English-only programs, some were English as a second language programs that were supplementary to regular instruction, others self-standing structured English immersion programs, also known as sheltered English. The American bilingual tradition, reinterpreted by government and education authorities, was succumbing to English monolingual instruction.

Bilingual Education Recast as "Dual-Language"

As bilingual education was capitulating, a movement to save some of it under a different guise was afoot. Now called two-way dual-language education or two-way immersion in an effort to silence the word "bilingual," the new proposal required that half of the students be learners of English and the other half be learners of the language other than English (Lindholm-Leary, 2011). This two-way dual-language movement coincided with the greater commodification of bilingualism in an increasingly globalized world. But in the way they were constituted, these dual-language bilingual programs were also mired in controversy; for they, more and more, appealed to white monolingual English speakers, leaving behind the ethnolinguistic communities who continued to desire a developmental maintenance bilingual education program for their children (Valdés, 1997). Also controversial were the regulations in many school districts that 50% of the students had to be of one kind, and 50% of the other; for communities, and especially the segregated ones that continue to be prevalent in the U.S., are not simply made up of equal number of different types of students. In addition, some minority ethnolinguistic communities felt cheated of an opportunity for bilingual instruction, for now 50% of the seats had to be filled by those who were English speakers, leaving them with only half of the prospects for bilingual education.

Eventually some communities developed what became known as one-way dual-language programs, bilingual programs that were meant for only one non-English ethnolinguistic group. A few school districts started immersion programs especially in Mandarin Chinese, Spanish, and French for their English-speaking students. Although immersion bilingual programs for white monolingual middle-class children are rare, they are not controversial. However, the bilingual education of ethnolinguistic communities with immigrant or racialized backgrounds continues to be controversial. And so, what are called one-way dual-language bilingual education programs, previously considered developmental maintenance bilingual education programs, continue to be seen with suspicion.

Language practices of white middle-class monolingual Americans are the only ones legitimized in U.S. public schools, with the others, stigmatized. Both one-way, as well as two-way, dual-language bilingual programs often fall short in legitimating the practices of bilingual Americans, for they have been built following an immersion pedagogy that might serve English-speaking majority children well, but that does not build on the entire language repertoire of bilinguals. In many dual-language bilingual programs, bilingualism is seen as a separate dual-language competence, a monoglossic view of bilingualism that relies on the conventions of named languages of nation-states, rather than on the unitary linguistic system of speakers. Bilingual speakers and those who are becoming bilingual, emergent bilinguals, are always translanguaging, that is, deploying features from their unitary linguistic system to successfully complete communicative tasks and acquire the social conventions that we call named languages—English, French, Spanish, Arabic, Chinese, Japanese, Italian, and so on (García & Li Wei, 2014; Otheguy, García & Reid, 2015). But many bilingual education programs, both two-way and one-way, fail to leverage the entire communicative repertoire of the child, limiting their performances only to those that are constituted with features of what is considered standard English-only or the standard language other than English-only. The linguistic practices that characterize bilingualism, often failing to conform to one standard named language or another are stigmatized and the children are not given the opportunity to extend those practices. Bilingual programs that act in this way only add to the linguistic insecurity of all bilingual children, no matter what type they are. Because they do not reflect the American ethnolinguistic communities, and are not led by them, the strict interpretation of what are understood to be separate dual-language competences only adds to the self-doubt of bilingual children and lack of confidence in their bilingualism.

Bilingual Education Making a U-Turn

As I said in the beginning, the most important contribution of Fabrice Jaumont's book is that it takes an approach to bilingual education that *returns the power to ethnolinguistic communities and their desire for the bilingual instruction of their children*. Bilingual education takes a U-turn that returns it to the direction in which it began—as a way of recognizing the communities' wishes to educate their children bilingually. Jaumont's book shows us how parents and communities are leading this U-turn.

The bilingual education field has focused on how programs ought to be constructed and how teachers ought to teach. But the most important component of bilingual education, the ethnolinguistic communities and the parents themselves, and especially mothers who have always had such an important role in their children's education, have been left completely out.   This is a book that educates parents so that they become the educational leaders and direct the development of bilingual education programs that serve their community and their children well. These bilingual education programs do not find their children's linguistic or cultural practices suspect. They honor the communities' funds of knowledge. The book tells the story of real parents that organize the community and battle to change the direction of American education today. We see how the partnerships that the parents build are not solely among themselves or with powerful organizations, but with others and other communities who have histories and experiences in the struggle. The greatest power it turns out is that of parents, interested and committed to the bilingual education of their children. This is not the usual parental participation or even engagement that the education literature talks about. This is about the leadership of parents who lead school change. The power dynamics are inverted, as it is the community itself that is in the driver seat, making the U-turn and leading the way.

It is interesting that this parent revolution is portrayed in this book as happening in New York City, a "multilingual apple" where Americans have always had different linguistic and cultural practices (García & Fishman, 2001). It is also interesting that it has been a scholar of French heritage living and working in the United States that has recognized (and in many ways spearheaded) this bilingual revolution. Jaumont's role in educating all parents to understand the benefits of bilingual education, as well as in supporting parents of all backgrounds in organizing themselves, has been without equal, for from the beginning he knew that only parents and communities could be change agents. The success of the American bilingual education tradition will rely on the willpower of parents. But willpower alone is not enough, and that is why Jaumont in this book gives parents a roadmap of how to start and support successful bilingual education programs.

As the book demonstrates, this parent-led revolution for bilingual education is not the same for all communities. Unlike dual-language bilingual programs mandated by local educational authorities that are all made from the same mold, this book leaves the design of programs up to the specific communities. Of course, these ethnolinguistic communities have to conform to certain mandates from school districts, but the ways in which they do so differ from community to community. In fact, one of the biggest takeaways from Jaumont's book is that despite the greater ethnolinguistic diversity today, it is possible to develop and sustain bilingual education programs for different communities. The efforts of the Arabic, Chinese, English, French, Japanese, Italian, German, Polish, Russian, and Spanish-speaking communities portrayed in this book have been different. Their actions have served their own interests, but also those that go beyond their own. Jaumont shows not only the successes of parents, but also their struggles and defeats, as well as how they have had to adapt to political and social pressures in order to survive.

Jaumont takes us in a U-turn, returning the design of bilingual education to families and communities, reminding us that this is where it all started, in the 18th century, as well as in the 20th century. Our experience tells us that creating bilingual education programs from the bottom up is not easy. But it is an important struggle, one that has always been part of the American ethos and that is being reclaimed today by communities across the country. This book, more than anything else, is a tribute to the hard work of parents and communities who have always made bilingual education possible, despite struggles and opposition. And in making visible the important role especially of women in this revolution— mothers and teachers who have always been caretakers and educators—we are reminded that the future of our American bilingual children is in good hands, in hands that refuse to give up their caring and supportive role to simply school bureaucracies.

The Call to Action

What if we lived in a world where every child could grow up bilingual? If this idea inspires you, then know that there is a way to do it. Through the hard work of parents and educators, a renewed push for bilingual programs is changing the educational landscape of schools, communities, and cities around the world. Over the last two decades, the American approach to education has gradually shifted away from the mastery of one language to the goal of bilingualism, language enrichment, and the preservation of heritages and cultures. This new approach has pushed linguistic communities to create dual-language programs that have embraced these new goals. The new programs have attracted thousands upon thousands of families who embrace multilingualism and have triggered interest among many parents who wish that they themselves had access to such programs in their local schools when they were younger.

Although the roots of bilingual education in the United States can be traced back to the early 17th century, a new phenomenon is emerging with three objectives. First, to espouse the cultures specific to families and linguistic communities, and to promote this cultural heritage as an important part of the mosaic of our society. Second, to help facilitate reconciliation between parents and schools, and encourage a fruitful dialogue between parents, school administrators, and education professionals. And third, to promote a social, economic and cultural environment that is respectful of all and helps to bridge the gulfs that divide us today.

Bilingual education means different things to different people. Some want access to English and the equal opportunity it provides. Others want to sustain their heritage, and utilize bilingual education as a tool to do so. Others are interested in the benefits of bilingualism for cognitive development. Others are interested in the acquisition of a second, third, or

1

fourth language because of the professional opportunities and advantages it will yield. Ultimately, these perspectives share the same goal: to create a multilingual society with greater access to languages and cultures. One of the main objectives of this book is to weave together these different perspectives, ensuring that more dual-language programs are created to generate greater opportunities for all children. Being bilingual is no longer superfluous nor the privilege of a happy few. Being bilingual is no longer taboo for immigrants who want so dearly for their children to blend seamlessly into their new environment. Being bilingual is the new norm, and it must start with our youngest citizens. By affording the advantages of bilingualism to as many children as possible, we can bring forth a viable 21st-century approach that will advance the growth of our societies by encouraging communities to invest in their linguistic heritage, by pushing schools to embrace dual-language education, and by raising new generations to be multilingual citizens of the world. This vision is reinforced by the belief that when quality bilingual education is available to everyone—in public schools across the country from preschool to college—our children's chances of success improve, our schools flourish, and our communities thrive. More importantly, the essence of this Bilingual Revolution is that it places parents at the center of change, as they have the power to transform the educational landscapes of their communities.

The parents that have spearheaded recent dual-language programs, some of whom provide testimonials in this book, value the benefits of bilingualism, biliteracy, and biculturalism. They ask that schools help foster multilingual competencies and encourage new language acquisition as early as possible, preferably through immersive programs. Some of these parents are also motivated by a strong desire to sustain their linguistic heritage and ask that schools place value on their children's heritage language and culture. As school authorities reconstruct bilingual education so that it serves more children and meets new objectives, the aim of this book is to empower parents to make a difference by forming initiatives and establishing new dual-language programs. This would be a huge benefit for any society whose citizens are willing to open their minds to the world—the world of others—by mastering languages and discovering new cultures. The Bilingual Revolution tells the story of a bottom-up, grassroots approach conducted through the efforts of parents that positively transformed schools and communities in unprecedented ways.

Where Do I Begin?

To succeed, parents should educate themselves on various aspects of bilingualism, bilingual education, community engagement, and the organization of volunteers. They also need to understand the partnerships that are required to build strong programs and gain the commitment of school leaders, the dedication of teachers, and the ceaseless involvement of parents at all levels. With this informed approach and sensitivity, parents and schools hosting these programs can benefit from the multifaceted population they serve. These programs also call upon the diversity of the teaching staff, as well as their ability to incorporate linguistic and cultural differences into their pedagogy. As this model is rich in cognitive advancement and beneficial to the brain's functions, the payoffs for our children and our communities are significant. The following chapters will discuss in greater detail these important findings and concepts, and lay out steps to follow so that more bilingual programs are established. Conceived as a practical and accessible guide to accompany parents and educators in their project, the Bilingual Revolution is the story of a movement born in Brooklyn, told through the eyes of parents and educators who founded bilingual courses in their schools. These parents were convinced that bilingual education is a universal good that should be offered everywhere, because it can constructively change a child, a school, a community, and even a country.

The roadmap presented in this book provides readers with the knowledge, shared experiences, and tools necessary to create effective dual-language programs. This roadmap was designed by both parents and educators so that others, like them, could grow and develop their own bilingual initiatives in all corners of the world. Inspired by the spirit of this movement, this book aims to encapsulate the energy and vision of parents and educators in New York City who saw the importance of dual-language education in an ever-globalizing 21st century. The drive and collaborative spirit of this motivated group fuels the Bilingual Revolution to this day, sprouting new initiatives in communities throughout the United States and around the world. While New York serves as the backdrop for this book, it is my belief that the roadmap can be applied to more than just large urban centers and that bilingual programs can flourish everywhere.

An Inspirational Success Story

With half of its population speaking a language other than English at home, New York City is a microcosm of the world that serves as a fitting backdrop for this book. New York is the ideal hub for a bilingual revolution. As the city serves over 100,000 children in 200 bilingual programs, New York accommodates a population of students with diverse language skills on a giant scale. Bilingual education is now offered in a variety of languages: at the time of publication, these include Spanish, Mandarin, French, Arabic, German, Creole, Italian, Japanese, Russian, Bengali, Polish, Urdu, Korean, and Hebrew. Many personal stories and accounts from these programs are featured in this book. Moreover, former Chancellor Carmen Fariña, who has been a strong proponent of bilingual education throughout her career, strongly encouraged the expansion of dual-language programs throughout the city during her tenure as Chancellor of New York City's Department of Education.[1] Her successor, Richard Carranza, seems equally determined to continue this development.

By establishing dual-language programs in public schools, the city collectively provides access to quality bilingual education to children of diverse socio-economic and ethnic backgrounds. Dual-language programs have been in existence for over twenty years in New York, and are gradually and successfully replacing traditional models of bilingual education that focus on teaching English to immigrants.

Former bilingual programs were generally offered in a transitional form, designed to help non-English speaking students become proficient in English while they continued to learn and receive content appropriate for their age and grade in their native language. This approach sought to facilitate students' transition into the English language and the general instructional program, but did very little to develop or even maintain the students' native language, some of whom eventually became monolingual in English. By law, many states in the United States require that a bilingual program be implemented if a school has an enrollment of twenty or more students with limited English proficiency in the same grade, assigned to the same building, with the same native language.[2] In New York City, when fifteen students speak the same language and are in either the same grade or two contiguous grades, a bilingual class must be established.

Beyond New York City

Similar programs have been developed in hundreds of cities in the United States and around the world. The Bilingual Revolution is a story of successes but also of setbacks, told through the testimonials of parents and educators. In their diversity, these portraits illustrate a viable 21st-century strategy to preserve a linguistic heritage and to raise a new generation of bilingual, biliterate, and multicultural citizens of the world.

Children and adults alike are part of this movement to preserve linguistic, cultural, and historical ties to their ethnolinguistic community. The desire for bilingual programs has swept through schools by storm. In 2013, 39 states and the District of Columbia reported to have implemented one or several dual-language programs.[3] This number is anticipated to multiply exponentially in the coming years.

Bilingual education has enormous potential. Why? Because our children are part of a world that is shrinking and in which languages serve as pathways to understanding others around the globe, as well as understanding who we are. Our children deserve the opportunity to connect not only with their relatives and friends, but also with their and others' culture and history. This learning approach has the potential to foster respect, tolerance, and mutual understanding. These are the cornerstones of a peaceful world.

We need to embrace and advance homegrown bilingualism, but that can only happen if we offer these languages in public schools. Furthermore, immigrant children raised in environments that value the language of their parents learn the dominant language faster, as many of the studies discussed in this book will show. Today, more and more students benefit from full-time dual-language programs in public schools and graduate fully bilingual, biliterate, and bicultural. An increasing number of language communities have now joined the Bilingual Revolution, as the examples presented in the book can confirm.

Some words of caution

Before moving on to the central idea behind this book, it is important to acknowledge the fact that this book does not pretend to cover all of the many extensive issues that surround, and sometimes plague, bilingual education—particularly in the context of public education in the United States. Issues of race, poverty, segregation, class, and gentrification have had and continue to have a significant bearing on the development of bilingual education programs and on public education in this country. We must be careful that these programs do not become exclusively for the privileged, and must continue to work in solidarity with minority communities that have the most to gain from these programs and the most to lose should their neighborhoods become gentrified. These issues need to be examined seriously and in much more detail than within the limited scope of this book. Many scholars and authoritative studies are cited for further reading throughout the book, and in the bibliography, to allow readers to dig deeper into these sensitive topics.

With the benefits of bilingualism and multiculturalism becoming clearer to researchers—in particular the impact of bilingualism on cognitive enhancement, critical thinking, and sensitivity toward other people and cultures—the Bilingual Revolution seeks to inspire and engage all parents to become bilingual "revolutionaries." These individuals will not just be advocates of bilingual education, but true pioneers willing to spur positive change in their societies and re-enchant the public with public schools, all while promoting an active community life (socially, economically, culturally) and a mutual understanding and respect for minority groups and people of varying sociolinguistic and economic backgrounds. This is the path to break the crippling cycle whereby access to good education is often linked to household income and status. The voices of revolutionaries old and new are heard throughout this book as their stories intertwine with the overarching theme of the Bilingual Revolution: a better future for our children and our world.

CHAPTER 1

The Willpower of Parents:
Yes, You Can...

A round the world, newly-founded bilingual programs owe much of their success to the sheer willpower of parents. In the United States, a large majority of dual-language programs were created simply because families asked for them or were able to convince the school's leadership of their advantages. Parents have long been strong advocates for bilingual education and have supported the implementation of dual-language programs with financial contributions, fundraising efforts, and volunteer work. This is not simply an American phenomenon; there are a myriad of international examples of initiatives launched by parents interested in bilingual education for their children, to either acquire a new language or preserve their linguistic heritage. What ties all these movements together is parents' overwhelming desire and commitment to bestow valuable skills and advantages to their children to help them succeed in an interconnected, global world.

Knowing Your Power

Historically, the initial foundation and implementation of bilingual education programs in the United States was a direct result of the dedicated work of civil rights activists—many of whom were parents themselves who wanted to ensure that their children were given the opportunity to learn at school and succeed in society—who fought to win court cases for recently-arrived immigrants who spoke little to no English in the 1970s and 1980s.[4] These parents successfully demonstrated that their children had a right to bilingual education, by highlighting the disadvantages of monolingual education for students who were learning English as a second language, and by demanding instruction in their children's' mother tongue in addition to English. Thanks to the pioneering work of these activists, parents across the

United States are now entitled by law to select the language acquisition program of their choice if enough parents in their public school community request to form a class.

The number of success stories of parent groups across the globe who have used their leverage to spur the creation of bilingual programs is truly remarkable. In France, where bilingual education is heavily regulated by the government, bilingual programs only began to appear in the early 2000s due to pressure from grassroots parent associations to promote the programs in private, and eventually public, schools.[5] In Ireland, although the government supported the teaching of Irish as a second language, it was parents who fought for bilingual programs in Irish and English throughout the country—even beyond the Gaeltacht areas where Irish is still spoken in daily life.[6] In Canada, a parent organization called "Canadian Parents for French" has become an important force for growth of bilingual programs nationwide, organizing French language advocacy campaigns and publishing reports on issues such as equitable access to immersion programs, accommodations for special needs bilingual students, and job prospects for bilingual professionals.[7]

If parents organize well and sustain their determination, even if faced with significant challenges, they can become a force to be reckoned with in public education. They have the potential to create access to bilingual programs for children of diverse socio-economic and ethnic backgrounds. However, as we are all aware, parents are not the only actors involved in educational communities. Therefore, parents must often collaborate with other actors at the school and community levels in order for a successful dual-language program to emerge. It can sometimes be difficult to garner the support of principals, teachers, and administrators who often are not bilingual themselves and are not necessarily knowledgeable about bilingual education. To be blunt, the burden of convincing school administrators and teachers of these programs' merits often falls on the parents. A former New York City principal of a school with both Spanish and French dual-language programs had the following things to say on the matter:

> Parents have the most power. Parents need to petition, and write letters, and complain because that will create change—far more than anything that I can do, as much as I or any other principal would want to and would try. It's the parents that really do have the power. Not that it's always successful, but they are able to get the

ear of the people who make those decisions.[8]

As this principal rightly notes, parents do indeed have an authoritative voice in public school communities and can attract the attention of key decision makers. Their power should not be underestimated.

What often complicates this leverage is that often school authorities can fall short in creating opportunities for community meetings where parents can discuss their thoughts on what specific programs and initiatives the school should implement. These types of gatherings can be extremely fruitful because they reduce the apprehensions that administrators and teachers may have about parent-led initiatives, and boost parent engagement and morale. The excitement, energy, and drive that parents bring to the table can be infectious. Meetings that bridge the gaps between parents and educators can help surmount various obstacles that both may confront when creating a bilingual program (i.e. by hearing from people who have successfully implemented programs of the same kind, or by creating a joint strategy or plan of action). However, in the absence of a receptive school administration, parents can be forced to take alternative and perhaps more confrontational routes in their efforts to create dual-language programs in their local schools. While complaining should always be used as a last resort to launch a dual-language program, it is sometimes the only way to initiate a dialogue with school authorities if the right channels are not in place to welcome and appreciate parent input. It is advised that parents be aware of their bargaining power and their rights, but always try to forge productive and cooperative relationships with other actors in their educational community first.

Parents need to be mindful that with any large change comes natural resistance, especially from those not engaged. Getting to know the larger school community is paramount to the success of each dual-language program. In New York City, for instance, many parents seeking to establish dual-language programs target schools in their district that could benefit from increased registrations or would welcome increased funding. These parent groups may appear to come from the outside, imposing their will on the existing school population, whether intentionally or otherwise. Parents should be very careful to avoid conflict with the school's existing parent base and take special care to integrate themselves into the larger fabric of the school community, beyond the dual-language program itself. Ensuring that all the benefits of having another cultural community within the school is extended to all students is imperative. This goal can be achieved by providing opportunities such as enrichment programs, field trips, and pedagogical resources to all children at the school.

Cultivating Community

Parents from diverse backgrounds and ethnic communities can become architects of bilingual educational opportunities that benefit their own heritage community. In New York City, a large majority of families interested in creating new dual-language programs near their homes are motivated by a strong desire to sustain their linguistic heritage that goes beyond a simple desire to develop English skills. Heritage language communities can strengthen the linguistic bonds that unite them by reinforcing and supporting dual-language programs. It is not sufficient to develop and sustain a language at home without oral and written reinforcement at school. Language loss and assimilation into American society occur rapidly, especially in children. Dual-language programs are ideal in that they provide a high percentage of daily instruction in the target language as well as in English, enabling children to improve upon their skills in both languages within an academic context. It is up to parents in heritage communities to ensure that their children receive this kind of education. It is their right and it is well worth fighting for.

For heritage language families, there are clear and proven advantages to supporting the academic development of their native language. For instance, if older members of the family, such as grandparents, speak a heritage language, a dual-language program can enable children to develop relationships with them across generational and language gaps. The benefits are even more pronounced for parents who speak languages other than English; dual-language programs allow children to develop deeper connections with their parents by conversing with them at ease in their native language. The problematic phenomenon of language loss is all too common in the United States. Time and time again, immigrant parents feel that they should not speak to their children in their native language because it will keep them from learning English, or are worried that their children's bilingualism will mark them as the subjects of discrimination. As a result, some families actively choose to speak in broken English to their children instead of speaking their perfectly fluent native language. This practice does not help, but actually hinders, children's overall linguistic abilities. Dual-language programs work to counteract these harmful practices by providing meaningful instruction in both English and students' heritage language in an academic setting, as fluency in one language reinforces fluency in the other.

Dual-language programs also present a rather unique opportunity to cultivate relationships among diverse groups of people within a community and to bridge traditional identity "barriers." As children from different linguistic backgrounds, cultures, and perhaps socio-economic statuses interact with each other daily in the classroom, families may eventually form friendships and relationships that cross these seemingly impenetrable boundaries. Furthermore, dual-language programs benefit the whole community by enlisting the help of motivated parents for school-wide causes, enhancing fund-raising capabilities and enriching the school's extracurricular offerings. Often, neighborhoods with newly established dual-language programs immediately become more desirable after the program launch due to the highly sought-after curriculum. This positively impacts the local economy and quality of life in the neighborhood, and consequently expands the programs themselves.

For many principals, a dual-language program is a way to leave their mark on a school by embracing the distinctiveness of bilingualism. Dual-language programs often have the power to save a failing school, improve test scores in all subjects including language arts and math, or give an under-utilized school a new identity.[9] One principal commented on their school's dual-language program in the following way:

> We opened the French dual-language program at P.S. 133 in a very organic way. In 2009, a group of Francophone parents asked me to consider the possibility of opening a French dual-language program. My assistant principal, literacy coach, and I visited a neighboring school with an existing program and decided it would be a wonderful addition [...] In 2010, I hired one bilingual teacher and opened one self-contained dual-language class. Let's just say it was a huge success. The following year, we opened two Kindergartens and one 1st grade class, and since then we have been adding two classes each year. Dual-language is a defining trait of our school, where students come from many linguistic backgrounds. The success of the French program encouraged the Hispanic parents to ask for a Spanish dual-language program. Five years later, I couldn't imagine a day without hearing French and Spanish in classrooms and in the hallway.[10]

In this case, parents not only convinced their school principal to create a dual-language program in French, they were also instrumental in the school's decision to offer a Spanish dual-language program. The efforts of dedicated parents effectively transformed a monolingual school into a model for dual-language education.

Building Success

Once established, parents play an immense role in supporting their school's dual-language program. Dual-language parents can act as ambassadors of their language and culture in their school's community by organizing cultural enrichment events or after-school activities and classes. It is very important to demonstrate that all the children in the school are being exposed to something of value and that it is not a privilege afforded solely to the students in the dual-language program. In addition, parents can provide much-needed assistance inside and outside of the classroom by reading aloud books to the class, assisting with the acquisition of bilingual classroom materials, cooking a cultural dish for the class to taste, or providing homework assistance for students who do not have a built-in linguistic support system at home, just to name a few ideas. Just as in a monolingual classroom, dual-language parents can volunteer as chaperones for field trips to enrich activities outside of the classroom in multiple languages. Marie Bouteillon, a former New York City dual-language teacher and a highly-regarded bilingual education consultant, describes the massive help provided to her by parents on field trips:

> What was so hard for me was that French was the minority language when I was teaching. When we went on field trips and everything was in English, having Francophone chaperones made a big difference. Having them paired with my English dominant students was fabulous. It opened their minds to something totally different, plus they were talking in French not in an academic setting but a social setting. That was really nice.[11]

There is no limit to the amount of support parents can provide to dual-language classrooms, and their commitment has the potential to ensure the program runs smoothly and achieves a high level of success.

In addition to much-appreciated and much-needed help, parents should also be very sensitive to not contribute any unnecessary stress, especially at the beginning of a program. Teachers and principals must both be given credit as capable instructors and administrators before jumping to any conclusions based upon personal opinions on how bilingual instruction should be carried out. As a bilingual curriculum is not developed overnight, parents must understand that teachers' work is extremely demanding and should appreciate the amount of effort that goes into building a dual-language program. Parents should reserve judgement on particular teaching styles, keeping in mind that dual-language instructors are inherently trying to navigate two or more distinct cultures, languages, and approaches to learning. This is no small task. The best way for parents to interact with the classroom is to encourage teachers, and offer assistance whenever it is requested.

Teachers greatly appreciate feedback regarding challenges that parents may be facing, as it is nearly impossible to anticipate potential obstacles parents may experience along the way. Instead of adopting an accusatory position, parents should allow their child's teacher explain the reasoning behind their choices in the classroom. Of course, it is perfectly acceptable to ask clarifying questions; however, putting teachers or administrators on the defensive after months, maybe even years, of planning for a specific program will likely not yield a positive outcome. It is important for parents to be considerate in their interactions with teachers and school administrators, as it truly takes special people to run dual-language programs. It is certain that they put the success of their class before anything else.

Once the program has gained momentum, there is a moment when parents—particularly founding parents—need to let go of their initiative and let the school take over. It may be difficult for parents to give up the degree of control they experienced to establish the program. This is a good time for these parents to think about how to continue to organize outside of the curriculum oversight and implementation role that the teacher will now assume. For example, parents could highlight places where the target language is not present in the school community and create new opportunities for that language to be practiced, such as inviting artists and authors to the school, hosting a cultural booth during a school fair, or organizing visits to local businesses, cultural centers, or museums where the language is spoken. Parents can become more involved in the school library by donating books, or managing the inventory, upkeep, borrowing, returning, and selections. Even small things around the school such as labeling multilingual signs in the hallways, or running lunch or after-school workshops for students, can be a huge asset to a dual-language classroom. Summer enrichment activities can be organized so students do not forget everything they learned in the previous year; sports, music, theater, and crafts, to name just a few activities, can all be done in the target language. These kinds of activities are ultimately what make the language learning process so fun and engaging for dual-language students.

Finally, another way to support a dual-language school is to engage in fundraising. In the dual-language context, it is important to consider that philanthropy might not be as broadly understood or even practiced amongst certain linguistic communities. This does not mean that a particular community is not generous or giving, but may rather have a different understanding of what is charitable and acceptable. Thus, motivating parents to become involved in a fundraising activity should be planned with a good understanding of the community's cultural way of giving. One group may feel comfortable writing a check or donating cash to help with a certain initiative, or the school more generally. Others might tap into their own network or appeal to their company. Some others may prefer to donate their time conducting research to find out how to obtain additional funds.

One of the most effective fundraising tools that is used recurrently by dual-language program leaders is their own non-profit organization, established by parents as a legal entity. This allows fundraising to take place outside of the parameters of the school.[12] This method can be particularly effective when a school is not in a position to authorize certain fundraisers, or does not want to be accountable to the district for the activities of a non-school support group. Parents can then donate money from the non-profit to the school for the purpose of purchasing new books, covering the cost of a field trip, or even sending a teacher to a conference, among many other things. This collective action has the power to ignite a spark in parents who know that they contributed to something tangible at end of the day.[13]

Some parents go beyond the call of duty and even decide to become dual-language teachers themselves. In New York, many parents have decided to go back to school to obtain their master's degrees in bilingual education because it is something they are passionate about and to which they want to commit their lives to. These kinds of personal commitments can ensure the longevity of a program and highlight the unwavering devotion to dual-language programs that exists in many parent communities. Parents are the wind behind the sails of each dual-language program—from the founding, to the implementation, to the long-term durability. Around the world, parents are realizing their potential to influence change in their school communities and to create bilingual programs that will benefit their children for a lifetime. If parents harness their power, there is no telling how far the bilingual revolution will spread.

Chapter 2

Changing the Landscape: Brooklyn's First Japanese Program

A fter hearing of several dual-language programs in New York City and Los Angeles public schools, five Brooklyn mothers decided they wanted nothing less for their children. As no such program existed nearby, they took on the challenge of creating a Japanese-English dual-language program from scratch—the first of its kind in New York City. The five mothers included Japanese Yumi Miki, Swiss-Japanese Monica Muller, Korean-American Hee Jin Kan, Taiwanese-American Yuli Fisher, and Chinese-American Lanny Cheuk. Yumi and Monica were the only two among the group who were able to speak Japanese fluently; the three others had little to no knowledge of Japanese, and no significant connections to Japan or the Japanese community. They met each other through a summer playdate group, Summer Hui, a subgroup of a well-known online network of parents in New York, Brooklyn Baby Hui. Through this summer group, these mothers organized playdates for their toddlers and gathered regularly in local parks. The five mothers became fast friends and soon got to talking about schools. They had heard of a successful French dual-language program that opened in a public school nearby, and began to imagine what a similar program in Japanese would look like. Beginning with these informal discussions in playgrounds and parks, the group started organizing and developing a plan to make their dream program a reality.

Fortunately, the moms shared similar views on multilingual education. They believed that exposure to other languages during childhood was important, and they understood the potential advantages and academic benefits of a strong dual-language program. Most importantly, they shared the same desire to change the school landscape, as one of the mothers beautifully described:

> We felt it would be easier to create our own program as a way to elevate another school in the district. The reason why it's so stressful for parents in New York to apply to Kindergarten or pre-

Kindergarten is that the disparity between the good schools and the bad schools is so large. We saw a dual-language program as a way to contribute to the school and the community, to bring a better education to more children, and to provide a bilingual education to our children. We wanted to change the landscape with the Core Curriculum, No Child Left Behind, and all the testing being used to assess teachers and schools. I thought, "What can I do as an individual to work around that and provide an education to my child that I think is better?"[14]

With this goal in mind, the group reached out to people who had experience in creating similar programs, including myself. Together, they worked tirelessly as a team and followed and adapted the roadmap—a condensed version of the one presented in this book—to fit their project's needs. Through it all, they understood that they were pioneers and that in order to succeed they would have to convince the Japanese community, school leaders, and a school community of the merits of their endeavor.

A Model is Found

The newly-formed Japanese Dual-Language Program group started out by exploring existing programs and researching effective models. They quickly found two public schools in Glendale, California, in the Los Angeles area, that had offered two-way Japanese-English dual-language programs since 2010.[15] The Glendale program was initiated by a number of parents who collected signatures and eventually went before the school district to request a bilingual curriculum. When they were granted approval, the program was inaugurated with one 1st grade class and two Kindergarten classes. At Glendale, half of the day is taught in Japanese and the other half is in English, by two sets of teachers. This is called the "side-by-side model." Approximately 40 percent of the school's population is fluent in Japanese when they enter the program. Some children have Japanese parents, some are Japanese-Americans, and some have no Japanese background but have parents who are very interested in Japanese culture, or who learned Japanese when they themselves went to college. When prospective parents tour the school, administrators make sure that these parents are truly interested in Japanese, as parents must commit their children to the full seven-year program, from Kindergarten to sixth grade. (Understandably, it is incredibly difficult for a school to replace children who suddenly leave after spending a few years in a dual-language program. This is, by and large, due to the fact that children who come to fill a spot at a later date must already have a good command of both languages to keep up with their peers who have been in a dual-language program since they started school.)

The Japanese dual-language program in Glendale teaches reading and writing in Japanese from the start, using hiragana characters in Kindergarten and adding katakana and Chinese characters in 1st grade. Although intensive and fast-paced, the program leaves room for fun activities and the use of technology such as smartboards. More importantly, students in the program have done very well academically. Five years after launching the program, the school conducted its own analysis of English test scores. From their data, the school found evidence that, after five years in the program, dual-language students outperformed students in monolingual programs in English.[16]

The school's Japanese language teaching staff is composed of Japanese natives, a few Japanese-Americans, and one teacher who worked in Japan and whose husband is Japanese. On the English side, monolingual teachers teach two alternating groups of students in English all day. English-speaking teachers do not have to understand Japanese—which forces students to only speak to them in English. The reverse is true for the Japanese language teachers. An advantage of the side-by-side model is that it reduces the number of target language teachers needed for the program. This helps manage the challenging task of finding qualified teachers who speak Japanese, have California teaching credentials, and are permitted to work in the United States. Additionally, the school hired a few advisors and university professors to help at the onset of the program. All these points were taken into consideration by the school's leadership team with the support of parents. Together they formed a powerful collaboration.

A Brooklyn Program is Formed

Our five mothers in Brooklyn used these valuable findings in Glendale to strengthen their argument and build their strategy. They also researched New York's Japanese community to gain a better understanding of which parents would be interested in the program. Yumi and Monica became the group's liaisons with the Japanese community. They were soon able to leverage the connections they made with local Japanese speakers to reach out to a large number of families that were interested in joining the program. This step was key, since having a critical mass of interested parents and eligible students is one of the most effective ways to convince principals of the need for a dual-language program.

With spreadsheets in hand, Yumi and Monica went door-to-door to Japanese community organizations to spread the word. They visited the Brooklyn Japanese American Family Association, a non-profit that sponsors Japanese cultural activities and offers weekend and afterschool programs, and Aozora Gakuen, a progressive school with a hybrid program geared towards Japanese families planning to stay in America. The group also reached out to the Japanese Consulate in New York and the Japan Society, a non-state organization whose mission is primarily cultural and educational.[17]

Different Audiences

One fact that the Japanese Dual-Language Program group soon discovered was that several private Japanese schools were already in existence, but tended to serve children of Japanese people who worked in New York before returning to Japan. These schools were modeled after schools in Japan, so that children of expatriates could maintain their language and were prepared to re-enter the Japanese school system when they returned to Japan. Because this system is already in place in New York, many expatriate families would not necessarily consider a dual-language program in a public school for a variety of reasons—the most significant being that dual-language programs do not usually meet Japanese school requirements or even their own expectations regarding the education of their child.

As a result, the group began to reach out to parents who were considering more permanent stays in the United States and who felt it important for their children to develop literacy skills in English. They also targeted families of mixed ethnic backgrounds, especially those with one Japanese parent and one American parent. These families were eager to ensure that their children maintained bilingual and bicultural connections to both countries.[18] The notion that students in a dual-language program could maintain one language while learning another was also very appealing to Japanese parents.

Surveying the community also brought to light some of the concerns that parents held about public schools, including the overall quality of public education in New York City, the food served in school lunches, or even the fear that children in dual-language programs would develop an accent in English or Japanese. In this initial phase of research, the Japanese Dual-Language Program group also found that some private schools were even becoming concerned that the new dual-language initiative was going to poach their teachers.[19]

The group found that if immigrant parents had no plans to return to their country of origin in the near future, they tended to look for a high-quality school with a solid track record of academic excellence to provide a strong educational foundation for their child's future. Consequently, the group discovered that certain parents were skeptical of the Japanese Dual-language Program project because it did not have an established reputation. This clued in our group that the Japanese Dual-Language Program initiative needed to devote energy to gaining the buy-in of uncertain parents.

It became important to recruit new parents on an ongoing basis so that the group could start to communicate on a larger scale. They used the internet to gather data through online surveys and to post information to keep parents updated on the progress of the initiative. A blog was created to meet several objectives:

> Our blog was created to get people on board while giving status [to the initiative]. We posted the roadmap and articles about the benefits of bilingualism, and we just tried to sell the program. None of us really had a blog before, so we just figured everything out. We tried to have a scrollbar on the side with the key points: who we are, how this got started, why we're doing it, what the school is, what we hope the program will be. You could also just get updates.[20]

Mass communication brought a lot of attention to the initiative, including from Japanese language media outlets in New York and Japan. From five mothers with a plan, the group attracted scores of interested families with enough children to launch an initial class one year sooner than expected. At the same time, they garnered even more interest for the ensuing classes. They also received many requests from families whose children were already in school, who were disappointed that their children were too old to join the program slated to start in Kindergarten.

Finding the Right Public School

Around the same time, the group started touring schools and looking for an administration with a curricular philosophy that would match their vision. The five mothers always visited the schools together and were usually granted a private tour. Lanny spearheaded the visits as she had the most experience working with schools:

> Having Lanny as an educator who is familiar with the Department of Education—she worked as a teacher—was very key. When we toured the school, she knew what questions to ask, what to look for in terms of curriculum, how the teachers interacted with the students, the administrative philosophy, and how the administration was. That was really a big help to us. We would not have gotten as far as we did without her knowledge.[21]

It did not take long for the group to find a few schools that they really liked, located close enough to where they lived. Their conversations with the principals also helped them narrow their choices down to two schools in North Brooklyn and, finally, one in Bushwick: P.S. 147.

After deciding on the school, the group immediately got down to planning with the administration. An initial concern of parents interested in the Japanese dual-language program, especially Japanese families, was fear of discrimination. At the onset, they wanted their children to all be in the same class. However, the five founding mothers responded with a compelling counter-argument: they did not want the Japanese dual-language program to come across as an elite segregated class of students. With the help of a few advisors, the mothers and the school leadership team developed a plan to integrate the dual-language classroom into the school, which included having students inside and outside the Japanese dual-language program meet regularly and participate in a weekly joint project. All of this intensive planning ensured that, as much as possible, no child felt isolated or deprived of the learning taking place in the dual-language program or the regular program.

As the initiative received overwhelming support sooner than expected, starting the Japanese program on a rushed time frame meant running into technical problems with the Department of Education's centralized registration procedure and adjusting to the general bureaucratic pace of the public school system—which was not always as fast as parents expected. Consequently, the initiative experienced delays that impacted the recruitment of families, particularly Japanese-speaking families who lived outside of the school zone. As a result, the first Kindergarten class did not start with the perfect 50/50 mix of Japanese native speakers and English native speakers as anticipated. This was a major source of frustration for the founding members that took quite a toll on the group's morale. In the end, only one of the original members of the Japanese Dual-Language Program group signed up for the program. The others declined due to personal reasons or moving out of the area.

Nevertheless, P.S. 147's principal, Sandie Noyola, resisted pressure to drop the initiative. Instead, she opened the program in the hopes that the bureaucratic difficulties would soon dissipate. A Japanese-speaking teacher with the proper qualifications and licenses was hired, and the program launched. A pre-Kindergarten class was established to attract both Japanese-speaking children and children whose families showed interest in the program, providing language and cultural content enhanced by the support of the Japan Society. With a balance of native Japanese speakers and native English speakers, a footing upon which to build the program began to take hold.[22]

A Gift for the Future

Parents, both veterans and new, have taken the lead in supporting and nurturing the Japanese program in Brooklyn. They worked tirelessly to establish a trustworthy reputation among Japanese parents and familiarized themselves with the registration process to aid incoming families in applying and understanding school zoning regulations. They supplemented the school's budget by establishing an associated non-profit 501(c)(3)[23] organization to benefit the school as a whole, both within and outside of the dual-language program. This project is ongoing. P.S. 147 parents' fundraising efforts have already allowed the school to invest in its students and curriculum by using the funds for things such as purchasing books, covering the cost of field trips, training teachers, and supporting enrichment programs at the school.[24]

The founding mothers' gift to society is incredibly important, despite the fact that most were unable to reap the benefits of their hard work. As a result of their efforts, New York's first Japanese-English dual-language program opened its doors in September 2015 at P.S. 147 in North Brooklyn. As we saw, the initiative faced great challenges, from locating a school and enrolling enough students in both languages to funding the program and maintaining interest in the face of major letdowns. Despite the setbacks, the spirit of the founding team was strong enough to push the program past the initial hurdles. Their exchanges of ideas, shared vision, individual commitments, and team efforts were instrumental in creating this unique program. Their initiative continues to progress as a new cycle of parents and educators nurture the budding program. Moreover, several Japanese parents in New York City and beyond have heard about the initiative and have been inspired to create dual-language programs in their own neighborhoods. In this way, our Japanese mothers have inspired others to create their own program themselves, and we have come full circle.

This shared passion and enthusiasm, as well as the proof that it is indeed possible for a group of five mothers to create such a program, have also inspired other linguistic communities to join the movement for bilingual education, as the following stories of the Italian, Russian, and German dual-language initiatives highlight. This is the quintessential story of the Bilingual Revolution. From the efforts and vision of a small few can come an entire movement to bring bilingual education to public schools.

Chapter 3

Summoning the Community:
Three Attempts for One Italian Program

M any recently-arrived parents in the United States are more than willing to take their children's education into their own hands, sometimes even leading by example when necessary. In their own search, a group of recently-arrived Italian expatriates came across the dual-language programs that other linguistic communities had been able to create across New York City. This began a long, and sometimes arduous, journey to inaugurate an Italian dual-language program in New York. These parents were Martina Ferrari, Stefania Puxeddu, Piera Bonerba, and Marcello Lucchetta. Their story illustrates many of the challenges and successes new initiatives can face. After not one, not two, but three attempts to create a program, the Italian community highlights the importance of perseverance for parents invested in their children's education.

Italians and Italian-Americans form one of the largest and most interconnected communities of New York City. According to the American Community Survey data, 85,000 people in New York five years or older spoke Italian at home in 2014, 30,000 of whom declared that they did not speak English very well. In addition to native speakers, there are also many Italian-Americans in New York City—especially in certain sections of Brooklyn such as Bensonhurst, Bay Ridge, and Carroll Gardens—who want to preserve their Italian culture. Census data from 2014 confirms that over 500,000 New York City residents reported that they were of Italian ancestry. However, despite these high numbers, the Italian Dual-Language Program group never thought that achieving a critical mass of interested parents to build the case for a dual-language program would be easy.

The Driving Force of 21ˢᵗ-Century Global Expatriates

The young and educated Italian nationals that made up the founding Italian Dual-Language Program group all came to the United States looking for prosperous employment opportunities and an exciting change of pace. Like many first-generation expatriates, they quickly adopted an American way of life and started having children of their own. Their work keeps them in regular contact with Italy and they speak Italian at home. This group of modern Italian immigrants return to their native land often with their children in order to keep their Italian roots alive. Christmas and summer vacations are important times to reunite with grandparents, visit cousins, and allow their children to be immersed in their native language and culture.

However, this group of parents found that even though Italian was spoken at home, as their children grew older, their mother tongue began to erode rapidly. This was due to the fact that they were surrounded by teachers and students who only spoke English in their preschools and communities. Additionally, at home, especially if one parent did not have Italian as their mother tongue, English might be spoken more frequently. The families made a significant effort to stick to Italian, as Marcello explains:

> With the younger children, we make every effort to feed them Italian, such as reading books in Italian and asking them questions to check if they remembered a word. Movies and cartoons help them absorb a little bit of language. Sometimes talking about differences like, "This is pasta the way we do it in Italy." We always make little comparisons of the way people do it here and the way that people do it in Italy.[25]

More complicated discussions in Italian required more time and patience from these parents, as their children's vocabularies in Italian was usually not as developed as in English. Often, their children had a tendency to reply in English to a question that was posed in Italian. Some children even developed a heavy American accent in Italian. Despite this, these dedicated Italian parents tried their hardest to maintain their linguistic heritage at home. In spite of their best efforts, they soon realized that their method would not be enough for their children to develop fluency in their native language, and decided that a dual-language program would provide the best opportunity for them to become comfortable in both languages.

The parents reached out to Ilaria Costa, the executive director of the New York Italian American Committee on Education, who in turn connected them with Lucia Pasqualini, the Italian Deputy Consul, and Carlo Davoli, the Education Attaché at the Italian Consulate. These contacts were able to spread word of the dual-language initiative to all the Italian nationals on the consular registry. Lucia also put the group in touch with Jack Spatola, whom she met during her regular visits to Brooklyn's Italian stronghold in Bensonhurst. Jack was the principal of P.S. 172 in Brooklyn and an active member of the Italian-American community. He was also the president of the Federation of Italian-American Organizations of Brooklyn, a non-profit charitable community service organization created through the efforts of dozens of organizations to unite, gather resources, and provide collective services to the Italian community and the City of New York. With these connections established, the group was now ready to test the waters and recruit interested families.

Within a very short time, Lucia and Ilaria set out to organize an informational meeting at the Italian Consulate. Flyers were distributed and announcements posted on social media, blogs, and via the consulate email database. Much to everyone's surprise, the community responded en masse; hundreds of RSVPs were received. An overflow room necessitated setting up a closed-circuit television at the consulate in order to accommodate additional guests. This impressive and enthusiastic response attracted the attention of the Italian media, who brought in cameras and reporters to cover the event. In the end, the meeting drew a crowd of over 200 people. The consulate's two main rooms were packed, with standing room only and overflow into the hallways. It was a victorious moment for the Italian initiative.

The meeting itself was organized in four parts. It started with a general overview of the advantages of bilingualism and dual-language education, presented by Bahar Otcu, a Turkish-American professor of bilingual education at Mercy College in New York. A panel of French, Japanese, and Russian parents who succeeded in creating their own dual-language programs then followed. The parents explained how they rallied their respective communities, recruited families, and presented their proposal to the schools they had selected. The evening continued with a panel of educators, including the then-director of the Office of English Language Learners of the New York City Department of Education, Claudia Aguirre, and myself. Finally, the last panel gave the floor to the parents who had initially contacted the consulate, as well as to Jack Spatola who generously offered his assistance. This portion of the discussion focused on the group's efforts to enlist parent involvement, as well as steps to take to convert the general enthusiasm for the initiative into one or more dual-language programs in Manhattan and Brooklyn public schools. The group also presented the blog that they had created, through which they intended to collect responses from interested families, disseminate information and updates, and coordinate school proposals. This ensured that parents could target the right school in the right area.

Assembling a significant number of interested parents is essential before approaching a school principal about a dual-language program initiative, but it is not the only necessity. Outside support from community organizations, additional sources of funding that are easily demonstrable, access to books and resources, and connections with teachers are also things to be considered when planning a new program. Without these, an initiative cannot succeed. This explains why, three years before the current Italian dual-language initiative was launched, it marked the end of a similar initiative led by an Italian-American mother, Christina Prostano.

The Trials and Tribulations of Grassroots Initiatives

Christina's great-grandparents immigrated to America from Italy in the early 20th century, but her family's ability to speak Italian gradually disappeared over the generations. Christina mourned that loss and hoped for her children to learn Italian, even though she herself only knew a few words. She tried to fill that void in her children's education, starting with a Facebook page and a survey to measure interest in learning Italian that attracted about 70 families, both English- and Italian-speaking. However, Christina was unable to meet the necessary requirements to launch a dual-language program, such as finding a school that had the desire and means to start the program, obtaining the support and funding of Italian organizations, and recruiting qualified teachers. Unfortunately, her valiant efforts to start an Italian-English bilingual program came to naught, and the initiative was abandoned.

Sadly, Lucia and Ilaria's group too faced obstacles in finding a school and maintaining the interest of the parents involved. Despite the initial enthusiasm they inspired, their initiative did not materialize. The loss of committed families as they approached the start of the school year and a lack of commitment on behalf of the public schools they considered was enough to quash the program. Their groundwork, however, helped trigger a new initiative in Bensonhurst, led by Jack Spatola and the Federation of Italian–American Organizations of Brooklyn, to open the first Italian pre-Kindergarten class in 2015. Unfortunately, this particular endeavor came too late for the children of the initial group of five parents, who were now too old to enter a dual-language Kindergarten class. When the founding group misses out on the opportunities they fought so hard to bring about, it is always a very frustrating moment for the families involved. Marcello describes this defeat:

> What I really would have loved is to have my kids in public school. We're here for a reason; there is a value in doing that. My dream was to have the dual-language Italian-English program in a public school. It was not just a matter of money, it was more a matter of knowing that there were other Italian-American kids like them and interested American families sending their kids to learn another language, which is my language. It was a dreamy view probably, a little visionary, but that was my first thought.[26]

It was also a loss for society at large, as the program would have served more than the Italian community by offering access to a beautiful language and an extremely rich culture to many children. As for Marcello and the other parents, they still hope for their children to speak Italian even if it often means that they, as parents, must teach them how to read and write. It is not a perfect replacement for a formal bilingual education, but it is what they have to work with for the time being.

Some also looked into a nearby private school in Manhattan, La Scuola d'Italia, although the high tuition rates and long commute time—particularly for families in South Brooklyn—discouraged many. Others hired au pairs from Italy, even though it required an extra room in the house and, often, a continuous yearly change of employment. Saturday programs also offered families a possibility for language exposure, some with the help of Italian organizations or the Italian Consulate. However, as is true with after-school programs throughout the week, committing to a Saturday program on top of an already very busy schedule can sometimes be too much to ask of a young child. These hurdles—in price, time, and lifestyle factors—illustrate the difficulty in maintaining a heritage language outside of the public education system classroom.

The Role of Heritage Communities

The original group's efforts, however, were not in vain. Their vision eventually came to fruition with the help of Jack Spatola, whose experience and school system connections led to the creation of New York's first Italian-English dual-language program. Instead of being carried out by newly-arrived Italian nationals, the initiative was now in the hands of second- and third-generation Italians. Interestingly, this new group's own families had been in similar situations thirty or forty years ago. They themselves had parents who spoke to them in Italian at home while they went to English-only public schools in New York. They witnessed the linguistic damage incurred within their own generation, or perhaps their parents' generation, and were remarkably able to mobilize in order to reverse the process of language loss in their community.

By and large, the Italian immigrants of this group's parents' and grandparents' generations came to the United States with little or no education. They had a very different background from our group of recent Italian expatriates, as many turned to jobs in desperation rather than seeking the "ideal" work situation. Unlike today's generation of Italian nationals in New York who are largely bilingual, previous generations had trouble communicating in English. Moreover, the Italian that they spoke was generally not standardized, retaining dialects spoken in their small villages which then crystallized once they came to the United States.

Today's Italian-Americans have the ability and luxury to make informed choices with regard to their children's education. Many heritage families have not maintained Italian at home, despite coming from previous generations of Italian immigrants. However, their desire to sustain their linguistic heritage has evolved with time. Jack Spatola explains:

> In my opinion, particularly within the Italian-American community, parents see the value of maintaining their heritage, maintaining the culture. I see that much more prevalent in young professionals. I see it as the need for maintaining the language and culture that before did not exist.[27]

For this new generation, language programs offered after school or on weekends were not sufficient means to attain their goals, to become connected to their linguistic and cultural roots, and to develop young bilingual Italian-American children. Jack confirms:

> The Italian-Americans, as well as many other ethnic groups

that have assimilated in the United States, have reached a particular level of understanding, of realization, of sophistication, of valuing their roots. Maybe because of a copycat mentality—"Others are doing it, why shouldn't we do it? We should do it too!"—or a real awareness. But, also, an understanding of the merit of a brain that has the ability to really think in two languages.

This enthusiasm for bilingualism and the many cognitive, professional, and social benefits it affords children throughout their lives has attracted much attention in the Italian-American community.[28] In addition to re-invigorating their cultural heritage and language, dual-language programs bestow upon children lifelong skills that they can carry with them, adding an element of personal development to the Italian community's quest for bilingual programs.

Success at Last

In 2015, with Jack Spatola's unwavering help, the Federation of Italian-American Organizations of Brooklyn teamed up with P.S.112 in Bensonhurst to launch the first Italian dual-language program in New York City. The team found an extremely supportive advocate in Italian-American P.S. 112 Principal Louise Alfano. When the program's opening was announced, the school received 270 applications for only twenty seats. Approximately 140 of the children were Italian-Americans whose parents wanted to preserve their precious cultural identity that had originated generations before, with even higher numbers expected for the following year. For the organizers, seeing so many families with young children interested in the dual-language program was enlightening; they always knew that there was potential, but they did not fully understand the incredible extent of the community's interest until parents started to sign up.[29] In a joint statement, the Jack Spatola and the Federation's President Carlo Scissura declared:

> The response from residents has been outstanding, and we have received many calls about these services. We believe that bringing dual-language programs to such a diverse community is vital, as they will help maintain different cultures while also generating a better understanding and greater respect for other ethnicities.[30]

It became clear that, despite past failures to launch a dual-language program, the community was now ready to support and embrace the initiative—and there was ample room for even more programs to develop and grow.

As we can see from the Italian dual-language story, it is not always easy to create programs from the bottom up. Their story sheds light on the unfortunate fact that founding parents sometimes miss out on the opportunities they worked so hard to create, simply because the program does not materialize fast enough to serve their own children. However, their story also illustrates the importance of perseverance, community connections, and the resilience of heritage language communities. This is not to be forgotten.

The desire to re-invigorate a linguistic or cultural community should not be underestimated, especially in the "melting pot" of the United States that holds many unique community histories. There are numerous multi-generational benefits in safeguarding a heritage, from preserving one's own literature, culture, and history to fostering a sense of belonging, pride, and identity as a member of a cultural heritage group. Dual-language programs enable heritage language students to sustain their heritage and develop new identities and skills of their own, in addition to becoming great sources of pride within each community. It is beautiful to see how this dual-language program has finally come to fruition within the Italian-American community of New York, with an outpouring of support among hundreds of interested families. As the saying goes, "If at first you don't succeed, try, try, try again." Each player in this story contributed to the Italian dual-language program's success—no matter how small their role or if they themselves were able to carry out their project in time. In the end, with a lot of perseverance, the right connections, and a little luck, bilingual education programs can and will succeed in transforming and revitalizing our communities.

Chapter 4

Strategic Minds: The Story of the German Dual-Language Initiative

In the summer of 2015, a group of parents at Kinderhaus, a German immersion preschool in Park Slope, Brooklyn, found themselves discussing elementary school options. Every parent in the group hoped for their children to continue on in both German and English. Some happened to be familiar with Sylvia Wellhöfer, a German mother who lived nearby and hoped to develop the first German dual-language program in a New York City public school. After making the connection, Sylvia and the Kinderhaus parents joined forces, with Sylvia and Celine Keshishian, an American mother of a bilingual child, taking the lead. To gauge interest among families in contact with the group, a kick-off event was organized a few weeks later. Project team leaders were appointed to help with the school search and parent recruitment, and a strategic plan was drawn up. The group was quickly joined by influential allies, notably Katja Wiesbrock-Donovan, head of the cultural section at the German Consulate in New York, and Andrea Pfeil, director of the language department at the Goethe Institut, a German cultural center. In addition to their expertise, these allies helped spread word of the initiative throughout the German community in New York's five boroughs.

German Roots in America

With increasing numbers of German-speaking families living in Brooklyn, the city recently recognized the need to include German in the school curriculum. New York City's German-speaking community is large and diverse, and is made up of Germans, Austrians, Swiss, Belgians, Alsatians, Luxembourgers, Northern Italians, and German-Americans. Germans actually represent one of the largest heritage language groups in the United States, and many Americans of German ancestry have a vested interest in maintaining their language and culture. However, keeping this heritage alive has historically been a challenge for the German community in the United States, since doing so used to carry many negative biases and prejudices. For those who came to the United States during the post-war era, this meant assimilating into American culture and possibly even hiding the fact that they spoke German, particularly for the sake of their children at school. This intentional suppression of German, and harbored post-World War II anti-German sentiment, impacted the way the German language was viewed and preserved in the United States, including in New York City. Fortunately, over time, this view has largely dissipated as attitudes have changed.

The current desire to maintain German culture in the United States emanates in part from German social clubs and societies that, from Queens and Long Island, down to Philadelphia, and up to Connecticut, remain active to this day. These groups organize events attended by third- and fourth-generation Germans. For example, Deutscher Verein—the second oldest German social club still in existence in New York City—was founded in 1842, its membership originally restricted to businessmen. It boasts illustrious members such as Frederick August Otto (FAO) Schwartz, Emile Pfizer, and the Steinway brothers. Although club members might not always speak German to each other in this day and age, they remain active participants in sustaining their cultural heritage.

German heritage in New York is now apparent in only a few traditional establishments, such as the butcher Schaller & Weber, the Heidelberg restaurant, or the Kolping House youth hostel. Saint Paul, a 175-year-old German Evangelic Lutheran church in Chelsea, holds services in German and continues to bring young families into its longstanding congregation. The Steuben Parade on Fifth Avenue, where thousands of German-Americans sing songs and dress up in traditional costumes each year, also epitomizes the celebration of German culture in the city. While recent expatriates from Germany do not always relate to these traditions, all acknowledge the role they play in the fabric of New York's German-American cultural heritage. German culture in New York is also currently witnessing something of a renaissance, especially in the restaurant industry, where younger generations have opened dozens of German-themed establishments in the last ten years.

Recently-arrived German families, many of whom are in the United States to advance their careers, are equally concerned about sustaining their language and culture. Several expatriate families in the parent group that did not plan to remain in the United States long-term began to consider extending their residency after hearing of the dual-language initiative, as they viewed local public schools as an excellent alternative to private German schools. This group of new immigrants represents an important part of the German landscape in New York, in tandem with the existing German heritage community.

There are interesting cases of organizations that bridge these two groups in the New York City German community. CityKinder, for instance, an online-based cross-generational community of German speakers in New York, organizes an annual Easter Egg hunt, summer picnics, the Steuben Parade, and Fall in the Park, an event where families gather for kite flying, baked apples on the grill, fall crafts, and story time. Their biggest event is the Saint Martin's Day lantern walk, when children make homemade lanterns and walk through Prospect Park singing traditional German nursery rhymes until they meet Saint Martin on horseback. To a certain extent, this organization has become a unifier for the German community in New York City, as German cultural centers, churches, and schools utilize it as a venue to promote their activities and reach younger families. It also played a critically important role in spreading the word about the German Dual-Language Program initiative—connecting families from various linguistic and cultural backgrounds to a project that had the potential to serve the community in unprecedented ways.[31]

The German Dual-Language Program initiative came to comprise a multicultural, multilingual, and multinational group. Like the borough of Brooklyn where they lived, they represented a wide range of ethnicities, professions, and interests, from entrepreneurs and managers to artists and students. Some of the families were monolingual English-speaking Americans. Some came from immigrant backgrounds—including those who came to make a life in the United States and others who eventually decided to stay. Often, families in the German dual-language group spoke English at home, regardless of whether or not it was their mother tongue. Everyone came from different religious and socioeconomic backgrounds. This diversity contributed to the strength of the German dual-language program.

Action

The German Dual-Language Program group's attempt to define a strategy from the start was an important factor in its success. The planning team used a "milestone" approach, setting deadlines and objectives to move the project forward in a timely manner. For example, the team decided that the group would need to choose a school by December in order to have sufficient time to register students by September of the following year. In addition, the outreach committee had to work ceaselessly to sell the program, as not all schools contacted were receptive to the idea or understood the benefits of dual-language education for their students and school community. For some school leaders, this was a challenge because it forced them to step out of their comfort zone.

Still, the group marched on, documenting the work that they would later present to the interested parents they represented. Sylvia Wellhöfer describes the first steps taken by her team:

> Initially, we followed the roadmap of the French program and adjusted when necessary. We did not define a district in the initial phase and did not focus on institutions as much as on the parents. We focused on creating a database to argue our case and determine the number of English Language Learners. Our database included personal information, but only a few people had access. This was very useful. After the kick-off meeting, we defined three sets of parents and reached out to the schools and decision-makers in the district. We compiled all the data in a joint document to be able to compare the schools and keep each other informed.[32]

The group's goal was to find fifteen German-speaking children and fifteen non-German-speaking before presenting their case to school authorities. To meet New York City requirements, they also needed to determine the number of children by school zone who were considered English Language Learners that would fit the program profile. The diversity of families interested in their initiative was a significant asset to achieving their goals, as children and parents had various levels of exposure to English and German.

From the start, the German Dual-Language Program group communicated regularly with all involved parties and developed a strategy to recruit parents who were committed to enrolling their children in the program. To find an appropriate school site, the group targeted three neighboring districts in Brooklyn and formed three independent working groups that researched each district and developed new suggestions tailored to each community based on the data that they had gathered. Although the group hoped to establish multiple programs in various neighborhoods over the course of several years, they did not want to compromise their initiative or misuse their volunteers' time and energy by trying to move in numerous directions at the same time.

With a target opening date in mind, the school search team had to make a final decision as to where to concentrate the group's efforts based on key elements such as the level of support from the school's administration and the availability of classroom space. The selected school needed to be easily accessible and prepared to handle the multitude of challenges that inherently come with the opening of a new dual-language program. The merits of each potential school visited by group leaders were shared with interested parents. The teams were also aware that under-utilized schools had the most to gain from a dual-language program, as these types of programs typically attract a wealth of new students and invested parents. New families are often eager to volunteer, help in the library, write grants, or acquire additional classroom resources. The growth in the school's population that customarily follows the establishment a dual-language program also guarantees additional funding from the City and the State Departments of Education. These factors, along with administrations' receptiveness to the idea of a dual-language program at their school, shaped the German Dual-Language Program group's decision-making process.

An Organized and Efficient Strategy

It was important for the German Dual-Language Program founders to be clear and upfront about their strategy at all times. Five private German schools in New York City were already in existence before the initiative began, three of which were in Brooklyn. The German Dual-Language Program leaders did not want to compete with these institutions or put themselves in a situation where their initiative would appear threatening to them. The group strongly believed that there was a need for a diversity of programs within the community, and saw their efforts to establish a dual-language program in a public school as complementary to the offerings of the private schools already in existence. The group was very careful to not amplify unnecessary tensions in an already challenging undertaking.

Depending on the individual families' needs, they even suggested the private school option first to some parents who could afford it. This collaboration and the backing of the private school programs ensured that a public school dual-language program would be a welcome addition to the community.

Our group knew that they had to build trust and maintain a vast network of contacts while remaining consistent in their strategy, following up on suggestions, and ensuring that individual requests from parents were taken into consideration. Sylvia Wellhöfer explains:

> I am very process-oriented. I am sure there is another way of doing it, but I always saw it as setting up a company or NGO without any funds. We launched a Facebook page and designed a logo and a website. When it was very important, I sent follow-up emails or phone calls. We communicated about the German Dual-Language Program via CityKinder, a German online platform, the German Consulate's newsletter, and the newsletter from the Goethe Institut. We also put up some fliers and tried to spread the word at playgrounds or functions that we attended. [33]

Parents regularly participated in open houses, met at local cafés, and conversed at the playground. The flow of information was constant. The partnerships the group built also reinforced the initiative's credibility and effectiveness. The Goethe Institut, for instance, offered to provide all classroom materials and reached out to its network of teachers for resources, curriculum development, and resumes. Connections were also made with schools that had more established programs such as the French dual-language program at P.S. 110 and the Japanese dual-language program at P.S. 147, in order to pass on lessons learned and useful tips for starting their own program.

When Disappointment Strikes

Thanks to the data they were able to compile and their clear communication with stakeholders, the German Dual-Language Program group was able to obtain an initial agreement from P.S. 17 in Brooklyn. Our highly-organized group of parents then sought out families that would enter Kindergarten at the same time, reaching out to groups in various school districts in Brooklyn and Queens. Unfortunately, a few weeks before the new school year began, it was determined that too many families had dropped out to meet the

September deadline. The German dual-language initiative at P.S. 17 subsequently did not materialize due to a reluctance on behalf of the school administration, as well as administrative hurdles that proved difficult to clear. In this case, as in most stories discussed in the book, it is important to secure commitment from parents and make sure they remain interested in the dual-language initiative. It is also important for group leaders to remain persistent and focused on finding a school, as this group did.

With the strong support of the district superintendent, the German Dual-Language Program team and the school leadership looked into several new options to open a German dual-language program. This resulted in beginning an after-school enrichment program in German for pre-Kindergarten and Kindergarten classes at a neighboring school, P.S. 18,, thus offering an opportunity to incorporate German content into the curriculum and maintain a link to German language and culture at the school. Much to their credit, the German Dual-Language Program team's efforts laid the groundwork for a German dual language program at P.S. 18. By staying true to its mission to bring a bilingual program in German and English to New York public schools, the group's perseverance is certainly exemplary and a positive indicator of more success to come.

The parents involved with the German dual-language initiative formed a well-organized group that designed a remarkable strategy to find schools and recruit families, and kept communications between parties clear at all times. They were open to attracting non-German speakers in the group. They were careful to work with private schools and cultural organizations as partners, not competitors. Although several families were frustrated that the program had to be postponed, much has been accomplished and hopes to see more German dual-language programs emerge in New York remain high. In an organized and well thought-out fashion, the groundwork for a successful German bilingual revolution has been prepared.

A Tale of Two Boroughs:
Russian in Harlem and Brooklyn

An event at Columbia University was the culminating point for the Russian Dual-Language Program initiative, led by mothers Julia Stoyanovich and Olga Ilyashenko. The meeting brought together an impressive array of supporters, including Tim Frye, a Russian-speaking American professor of East European studies; Maria Kot, a Russian native who helped save and build upon Russian dual-language programs in Brooklyn; and Tatyana Kleyn, professor of bilingual education at the City College of New York, who came to the United States as a young Russian-speaking child from Latvia and had to re-learn Russian as an adult. The gathering also included important state and city officials such as Luis Reyes of the New York State Board of Regents and Milady Baez, Deputy Chancellor for the New York City Department of Education, as well as school principals, teachers, representatives from cultural organizations, press, and parents. This gathering was but a small representation of a tremendous multi-year effort to create a Russian dual-language program in Manhattan's Upper West Side. Through many ups and downs, successive groups of parents tried for years to convince school authorities that a Russian dual-language program was needed in their part of the city. In the face of continued challenges, this call for action unified a very diverse set of individuals and expectations.

A Globally-Minded Linguistic Community

Not all the individuals in the room came from Russia. In fact, only a few did. Many lived in New York City but grew up in Russian-speaking homes. Others came from former republics of the Soviet Union or other European countries. When asked what other languages were spoken at home, families who advocated for the Russian dual-language initiative responded with Italian, Greek, Ukrainian, Tatar, Armenian, Spanish, French, German, Hebrew, Hungarian, Serbian, and Urdu, in addition to Russian and English. The assembled group represented 125 families with 160 children born between 2011 and 2016, or approximately thirty to forty children per birth year, who would soon enter pre-Kindergarten or Kindergarten. Many parents were native or heritage Russian speakers, although some spoke limited or no Russian at all. According to the organizers' data, about half of the children whose parents were interested spoke Russian at home; a quarter spoke English and Russian equally; and another quarter did not speak Russian, including English monolingual students. The group represented by this initiative was, as the mothers beautifully put it, as diverse as the city they inhabited: multilingual, multicultural, and eager to access new opportunities for their children.

Testimonies gathered from the families involved speak to the importance of a Russian dual-language program in their personal and family lives. A few parents struggled to learn Russian as a second language later in life and did not want their children to have to suffer as they had. Some children came from families with one Russian-speaking and one English-speaking parent, which made communicating in Russian at home an often challenging task. One family even had a child who was already trilingual in English, Russian, and Chinese, and wanted to enroll their son in a dual-language program so that he could master literacy in two out of his three spoken languages.

Parents highlighted the cultural benefits that both Russian-speaking children and non-Russian-speaking children would derive from the program as they discover the "treasures" of Russian culture. Founder Julia Stoyanovich's family noted that they spoke entirely in Russian at home because she and her husband wanted their son to be able to not only understand but also tell jokes and laugh in their native language. They also wanted their child to be able to communicate at ease with his grandparents who lived in Queens, Moscow, and Belgrade, and who spoke limited English. Many families self-identified as global Russians, a term that indicates a combination of Russian language and culture, a well-stamped passport, and a Western education and way of life. These parents believed that a Russian dual-language program would be invaluable to them as a means of preserving their identity, in passing on their native language and culture to their children.

The message of this diverse group was deep yet simple: E Pluribus Unum.[34] Their overwhelming hope was to combine their varied backgrounds and interests to create a thriving dual-language program. On the Upper West Side, where the initiative is based, it is not uncommon to hear Russian spoken on the streets. In fact, New York City has the largest population of Russian speakers in the United States. According to a recent census, the city had over 200,000 Russian speakers, making Russian the fourth most commonly spoken language in New York City after English, Spanish, and Chinese.[35] Approximately 3,400 Russian-speaking children in New York are identified as English Language Learners and qualify for bilingual education services. Many more students who come from Russian-speaking homes may enter school speaking some English, but need to become proficient in English reading, writing, and comprehension.[36]

Additionally, children of all language backgrounds, including English monolinguals, could benefit from a Russian dual-language program because of the importance of Russian on a global level, as well as the many hidden cultural, professional, and personal avenues it unlocks for fluent speakers. The founders spoke at length about their desire to share their love for Russian language and culture with others in the New York City community. They believed that the Russian program would be a gift to their children, but also to the greater community, and they were prepared to go to great lengths to make their dream a reality.

Fighting to the Top

Before we return to our two mothers in Manhattan, it is important to tell the original story of Russian dual-language programs in New York, a story that begins in Brooklyn. There, Maria Kot, a Russian-speaking parent, had become a key advocate for Russian bilingual education for her daughter and hundreds of other bilingual students at P.S. 200 and I.S. 228.[37] Maria organized community events and meetings, developed plans of action, and liaised with many advocacy groups, community boards, Russian families, and government agencies. She is now the parent representative at the New York State Association for Bilingual Education, where she is able to voice the interests of parents from diverse linguistic communities.

Maria's first interaction with Russian dual-language programs was when she enrolled her daughter at the elementary school level at P.S. 200.

Although the program was already in existance, just a few years into Maria's daughter's education it was on the verge of being cut when a new principal took over and other minority groups in the school felt that they and their children were not a part of it. Maria explains how difficult it was to convince parents and administrators of the need for such a program to continue:

> At that time, the situation was different and the idea of dual-language was not very welcomed. We had to fight. We had to start a fight with the Department of Education for our kids to have dual-language education. If that can be avoided, it should be avoided because it is stressful for everyone and you shouldn't have to do it.[38]

Following an exhausting legal battle with the Department of Education, Maria and the Russian dual-language program parents eventually won the right to keep the dual-language program for her daughter and the rest of the dual-language class.

Their argument centered on the past precedent of *Lau v. Nichols*, further explored in Chapter Thirteen, and the right of English Language Learners to have access to dual-language education. With proven documentation of the number of English Language Learner students, Maria was able to save the Russian bilingual programs in Brooklyn. Over time, the program continued to grow. A second Russian dual-language program opened at the middle school level, at I.S. 228, to accommodate the rising bilingual classes. This program was much easier to implement, thanks to an exceptionally supportive principal, as Maria describes:

> That was much easier, and peaceful, and more successful. I found a principal who was interested in improving his school. I reached out to him and explained the opportunity that dual-language could offer his school. It took a few visits before he actually understood the idea of bilingual education. But he then became an amazing supporter of dual-language. Since then, he opened a Russian dual-language and a Chinese dual-language program. The next year, he opened a Spanish dual-language program and then a Hebrew dual-language program. Now, we have the huge support and advocacy of the principal to continue.[39]

Incredibly, Maria's efforts to expand Russian bilingual programs afforded other linguistic communities the opportunity to implement their own programs. Moreover, P.S. 200 was designated a Model Dual-language

School by former New York City Schools Chancellor Carmen Fariña for the 2015-2016 school year. These successes demonstrate the power of parent involvement, as each initiative has the potential to change the educational landscape of a community.

Make Your Dream a Reality

Meanwhile, while Russian programs achieved significant success in Brooklyn, the Manhattan initiative continued to stall. All were well aware that previous attempts to create a Russian bilingual program in Manhattan had failed. But for Olga and Julia, this was not seen as a reason to give up. Instead, they rallied interest around their enthusiastic call to action. Julia describes their vision as follows:

> This is our dream. Our dream is very close to home. It is to establish a Russian dual-language program at a public elementary school on the Upper West Side of Manhattan. We want this to be a high-quality bilingual program. This program should help Russian-speaking English Language Learner children to learn English in a constructive, stress-free, and pleasant environment. It should also help children who do not speak Russian to learn the language and to enjoy and appreciate it together with us and with the rest of the Russian-speaking community and world. We want this program specifically to be at a public elementary school. We feel that the public school system is going to provide for us the benefits that New York City gives—the multiculturalism, the diversity, the integration, and the beauty of the city that we are happy to call our home.[40]

In addition to their own Russian-speaking community, our mothers developed a strategy to attract non-Russian speakers to their program based on three key things: bearded men, rocket ships, and the seal of biliteracy. Through her laughter, Julia described how the Russian language opens the door to Russia's rich cultural traditions, including the likes of bearded men such as Leo Tolstoy, Tchaikovsky, and Chekhov. The rocket ship, an ode to Sputnik, focused on career opportunities and job growth in the political, technological, and scientific fields in the Russian-speaking world. And finally, in a few select states including New York, the seal of biliteracy is awarded to high school graduates who have attained a high level of proficiency in one or more languages in addition to English, thereby lending legitimacy to dual-language programs across the country.

Many of the ingredients necessary to create a successful dual-language program on the Upper West Side were already present the night of the Russian Dual-language Program presentation. The group needed motivated parents and many of them were in the audience. They needed resources, both from the New York City Department of Education and from outside partnerships and organizations, many of which had representatives in attendance and among the presenters. They needed to identify highly-qualified teachers, and could do so by working in collaboration with the schools that they had already started to contact. The final ingredient was the students, guaranteed by the enthusiastic and committed parents in the audience. However, administrators in the audience and on the panel reminded the new leaders of the Russian dual-language initiative of the importance respecting and integrating into an already established school community. They urged the group to work with parents at schools who may feel threatened by change and new offerings. A hallmark of the Russian initiative, these moms expressed their resounding commitment to avoiding the creation of an isolated bubble within the school for the Russian language students. They were determined to construct a program to benefit the entire school community. As the group well understood, when a dual-language program is built upon respect, appreciation, and cooperation, the school becomes the foundation upon which a community can prosper.

The two sets of Russian dual-language initiatives, one in Brooklyn and the other in Manhattan, provide contrasting tales yet yield similar advice. In Brooklyn, what stemmed from a tough legal battle grew into a flourishing dual-language haven that embraces and strengthens its diverse community to this day. In Manhattan, the multi-year uphill battle to secure a school location in prime real estate has proven too daunting and difficult to establish a bilingual program for the numerous eager Russian families. At the time of this writing, the Russian dual-language initiative in Manhattan was in conversation with a school in Harlem that seemed open to its dual-language program proposal. Although the Brooklyn and Manhattan projects followed different paths, both champion the diversity of their communities. They seek to promote the various cultures encapsulated in their linguistic community, while sharing and celebrating their traditions with the greater public. In the end, whether their children are telling jokes, dancing in ballets, or reading Tolstoy, the Russian dual-language families in New York are committed to preserving their unique cultural heritages in their multicultural city, and to making their dreams come true.

Chapter 6

The Domino Effect:
Multiplying French Programs

It all started in April 2006 when three tenacious mothers walked into principal Giselle McGee's office at P.S. 58 in Brooklyn's Carroll Gardens, hoping to convince her that a French after-school program would be a worthy addition to her school. Like these mothers, many French-speaking families in the neighborhood were looking to sustain their children's French outside the home. Little did the French community know that Giselle would not only accept the after-school idea on the spot, but that their conversation would lead to New York's first French dual-language program, and the avalanche of programs throughout the city that followed. The French dual-language story in New York highlights the powerful domino effect of the Bilingual Revolution. Behind the force of a committed and motivated community, dual-language programs can multiply to serve ever-growing populations of bilingual students.

The Influence of Supportive Advocates

Until the age of five, this instrumental principal Giselle was bilingual, speaking French at home with her mother and English with her father. It was only when she started Kindergarten in Staten Island that she abandoned her French skills, as none of her classmates spoke French. Giselle grew up in the 1960s, when assimilation was prioritized in recently-arrived immigrant communities. Elementary schools did not even offer foreign languages at the time, meaning that children could not build upon their home language in the classroom if they spoke a language other than English. This is how five-year-old French-speaking Giselle lost her mother tongue. It is a story all too common in the United States of decades past, and a phenomenon that recent trends in bilingual education are attempting to reverse.

With her own story in mind, Giselle enthusiastically inaugurated the French dual-language program at P.S. 58 in 2007. The positive encounter between the three mothers—Catherine Poisson, Anne-Laure Fayard, and Mary-Powel Thomas—and their committed principal paved the way for numerous groups to replicate their efforts. Following the lead of this original group, new parents organized themselves into a critical mass—receiving the support and commitment of key community stakeholders and school administrators. This movement led to the creation of dozens of French bilingual programs throughout New York City, as well as in several other cities across the United States, over the last ten years. The ongoing success of P.S. 58's program encouraged new waves of parents to approach schools with French dual-language proposals, ready to do whatever it takes to bring bilingual education to their local neighborhoods. To this day, educators and researchers in the U.S. and abroad point to this particular program as a shining example of the power of dual-language programs in the 21st century.

As other communities in the city began to hear of P.S. 58's success, a growing synergy emerged between several organizations. These included the Cultural Services of the French Embassy, several non-profit and philanthropic organizations, local French-language news magazines,[41] and *Education en Français à New York*, a volunteer-based organization whose mission is to provide French offerings in neighborhood public schools. This dynamic collaboration facilitated the multiplication of the number of French dual-language programs in New York in a remarkably short period of time. It planted the seeds for the original bilingual revolution in New York City in what would come to be known as the "French Bilingual Revolution."[42]

The Public School Option

This revolution was propelled by a growing interest in bilingual education among the French-speaking community, compounded with a need to serve its diverse populations within the public school system. In 2012, I estimated that 120,000 people in New York spoke French at home, including 22,000 children—revealing a potential to fill over 50 French-English dual-language programs in the city.[43] In the New York metropolitan area, French-speaking expatriate families—as well as American and international families interested in French education—who can afford private school tuition have excellent educational offerings to choose from. Well-established institutions such as the Lycée Français of New York, the United Nations International School, the Lyceum Kennedy, the French-American School of New York in Larchmont, the International School of Brooklyn, the *Ecole Internationale de New York*, the French American Academy, and the French American School of Princeton provide high-quality bilingual education programs following accredited curricula in compliance with France's own national educational standards. In these schools, families enjoy the benefits and opportunities provided by bilingual education—for a price—and their children are able to master both English and French at a very high level.

In the early 2000s, New York saw an influx of young French-speaking families who could not afford to pay these schools' tuition fees. At the same time, several neighborhoods in West Brooklyn, Harlem, Queens, and the South Bronx witnessed a steady increase in their Francophone populations, including immigrants from Europe, Canada, Africa, and the Caribbean. These newly-arrived populations hoped to maintain their children's language skills while adjusting to life in the United States. This led to a massive growth in demand for French dual-language programs, spurred by the presence of French speakers who often went unnoticed by school authorities, as many also spoke other primary languages at home such as Wolof, Bambara, and Creole, and were identified as speakers of those languages only by school officials. French dual-language programs also became extremely popular among American and international families whose dominant language was not French, but were enticed by the idea of bilingual education for their children.

Growing the Revolution

The programs that opened in 2011 at both P.S. 110 in Greenpoint and P.S. 133 in Boerum Hill receive hundreds of applications each year for the small number of seats available in the French dual-language Kindergarten classes. These programs were initiated by parents of French heritage, some born in the United States, others in Canada or France. The majority of applicants are from English-speaking monolingual families with no cultural or linguistic ties to French. At other schools in Brooklyn, such as P.S. 20 in Clinton Hill and P.S. 03 in Bedford-Stuyvesant, the French dual-language program was actually initiated by either American parents who did not speak French or educators who wanted to improve offerings for underserved families from French-speaking countries.

Motivated parents like Virgil de Voldère and Susan Long, a French-American couple who wished for their two sons to be fully bilingual and biliterate, were inspired to launch a French dual-language program at P.S. 84 on the Upper West Side of Manhattan in 2008. Virgil explains how his own initiative started:

> My wife Susan proposed this idea of doing a French dual-language program. We all got together and started planning on opening the program the following September. This was February. By May, we had gathered information from 100 families in the neighborhood. Robin Sundick [then principal of P.S. 84] worked with her hierarchy to cut all the red tape. By September, by some miracle, we had a program. What I tell all the Francophone parents, and especially parents coming from France who are used to a state-run educational system, is that in America they can really make a difference. They can organize, they can propose, and they have a right to have their heritage language spoken at school.[44]

To achieve their goal, Virgil and Susan enlisted the help of another parent at the school, Talcott Camp, an American civil rights attorney, mother of two, and Francophile who hoped for her own children to become bilingual. She later became the president of *Education en Français à New York*. She explains her own participation in the initiative as the following:

> I was interested in language acquisition but, really, the reason I wanted a dual-language program for my kids was that I didn't want them to grow up monolingual. It just seems so impoverished. I wanted them to grow up with more than one language, for the richness of it and for the perspective it would give them on politics and culture—even mentally. We would have loved a French dual-language program but it just didn't occur to me that it could happen. It was really Virgil who said *"Pourquoi pas?"* ["Why not?"]. The principal at the time, Robin Sundick, said to him, "If you bring me enough Francophone families, I will do it." And that's when the work started.[45]

As promised, Virgil, Susan, and Talcott delivered the necessary numbers to make their French immersion vision a reality. The school they chose, P.S. 84, happened to be a pioneer in dual-language Spanish education, and was able to mobilize their existing dual-language administrative structure to quickly and efficiently open the French program in September 2008. Today, the program serves approximately 250 students with origins from Europe, Canada, the Caribbean, and Africa. By the end of 5th grade, all dual-language students are bilingual and biliterate, with a firm grasp of Francophone and American cultures. This success was made possible because of parents, who canvassed the neighborhood, designed posters, updated websites, and organized open houses.

Since September 2007, fourteen public schools in New York have opened French dual-language programs, ten of which are still in operation. The four programs that ultimately closed failed because of poor planning or a change in school leadership—significant hurdles to clear in the implementation of dual-language education. The success stories include seven dual-language elementary school programs, including public schools in Manhattan and Brooklyn and the New York French-American Charter School, a charter school in Harlem. Additionally, three middle schools offer a French dual-language curriculum through the 8th grade: M.S. 51 in Park Slope, M.S. 256 on the Upper West Side, and the Boerum Hill School for International Studies in Brooklyn. The latter is currently in the process of implementing the first French dual-language International Baccalaureate program in a public school in the United States, with plans to take dual-language students all the way to 12th grade, culminating with a bilingual International Baccalaureate diploma.

As more and more students in the French dual-language program are now entering high school, it is crucial that schools ensure the continuum of their education in both English and French. New York City's French dual-language programs currently serve over 1,700 students—with estimations of the total number of students served as nearly double that amount if one includes families that have relocated or dropped out, or programs have closed, since 2007. Current projections indicate that an additional 7,000 students could benefit from these programs by 2020, if the current wave of momentum continues to gain the support of new school principals, community members, and parents.

Growing Pains and Managing Success

Regrettably and perhaps peculiarly, the French Bilingual Revolution is hindered by a lack of access to space rather than a lack of interest. As a result, more families—both French-speaking and otherwise—have been turned away than have been accepted into French dual-language programs.

The number of seats available across the city remains limited, generating fierce competition among applicants. Fortunately, this problem can be combatted. Through partnerships with new schools and the engagement of new parents, the expansion of French dual-language programs can render these opportunities more accessible to eager families in New York City and beyond.

Still, classroom space is not the only problem that limits the development of these programs. As the number of French dual-language programs continues to grow, so does the need for qualified teachers. This predicament is often accompanied by various hurdles in recruiting competent, credentialed, bilingual teachers to work in public schools. At present, the majority of candidates for bilingual teaching positions in the United States are American citizens or green card holders, as schools are often unable to grant work permits to teachers from abroad due to complicated bureaucratic procedures. A degree in bilingual education is often required, and in New York City it is mandatory to have New York State certification to teach in a public school. Attracting exceptional teaching candidates in large numbers has become a crucial element in establishing bilingual programs. As a response to this need, Hunter College in Manhattan, which has offered a master's degree in Spanish bilingual education since 1983, added a French track to its course offerings. To encourage students to apply to Hunter's program and similar programs throughout in the city, the *Société des Professeurs de Français et Francophones d'Amérique* established a scholarship program to support new prospective French dual-language teachers.[46] Scholarship and certificate programs such as these are critical to dual-language programs becoming self-sustainable in the future.

In addition to qualified teachers, there is also a great need for educational materials, especially classroom and school library books adapted to different subjects and skill levels. Fundraising has assumed an important role in meeting these needs. Parents with experience managing campaigns and large-scale finances have been instrumental in raising the required funds to support schools that house French dual-language programs. A team led by professional fundraisers and dual-language parents assisted the Cultural Services of the Embassy of France and its partner, the FACE Foundation, in setting up a city-wide, multi-year fundraising campaign to serve larger numbers of French dual-language children, particularly in underserved neighborhoods in the Bronx, Queens, and East

Brooklyn where many Francophone families reside.[47] The initiative has now morphed into a nation-wide program, the French Dual-language Fund, under the leadership of Bénédicte de Montlaur, Cultural Counselor of the Embassy of France. Its aim is to build an enduring network of dual-language and immersion programs anchored firmly within the American educational landscape. The fund has received the support of generous individuals, foundations, corporations, and public institutions. Additionally, organizations such as the French Institute Alliance Française, the Committee of French-Speaking Societies, the Alfred and Jane Ross Foundation, the Quebec Government Delegation, and even the French Senate—thanks in part to the support of senators representing French citizens residing outside of France—all became ardent supporters of and generous advocates for the New York City French dual-language programs.[48]

Jane Ross, an international educator and former English teacher at the Lycée Français of New York, was also instrumental in establishing the French Heritage Language Program, hosted by the French Embassy and FACE Foundation. Over the last ten years, this program has helped young immigrants of French-speaking backgrounds preserve their linguistic heritage while adapting to life in the United States. It offers free French classes through the Internationals Network for Public Schools, an organization that welcomes newly-arrived immigrants.[49] Most of the students enrolled in the program hail from West Africa and Haiti. Through after-school and in-school support, the program builds upon the students' French literacy and accelerates their mastery of English. Students also have the opportunity to earn college credits by passing selective examinations while in the program. All in all, more than 3,000 students from Kindergarten to 12th grade have benefitted from the French Heritage Language Program since its creation in 2006. The program has become an integral part of Francophone education in New York and an important partner for dual-language programs, as well as a key player in the French Bilingual Revolution.

The synergy of the New York French dual-language program story perfectly illustrates the critically important role of parents and educators in the development of dual-language programs, as well as outside organizations that can provide critical support in a variety of ways. These vignettes are evidence that invested individuals can join forces to respond to a community's needs, establish successful fundraising campaigns, and create partnerships with institutions that have the capacity to provide assistance in solving problems that are simply too extensive and complex for a parent group to solve alone.

As we have seen, thousands of children have benefited from the combined efforts of many individuals, groups, and organizations devoted to French bilingual education in New York public schools. Hopes remain high that even more children will be served in the near future. The French dual-language story represents everything the Bilingual Revolution has to offer: quality programs in public schools for children of all ethnic, linguistic, and socioeconomic backgrounds. If the Bilingual Revolution continues to spread at this incredible rate, there is no telling how far it will go.

Chapter 7

Overcoming Prejudice:
The City's Arabic Dual-Language
Programs

The first Arabic-English dual-language program in New York City was founded at the Khalil Gibran International Academy, a public school in Brooklyn that opened its doors to sixty 6th-grade students in September 2007. The school's namesake, Khalil Gibran, was a Lebanese-American artist, poet, and writer of the New York Pen League. Gibran came to the United States as a child, growing up in Boston and attending school in a special class for immigrants. There, he was able to master the English language while maintaining his Arabic fluency at home. Gibran went on to become a well-regarded and celebrated literary figure in both languages and an internationally respected proponent of multicultural understanding, the embodiment of the spirit of dual-language education to this day.

The Khalil Gibran International Academy was the first public school in the United States to offer a curriculum that emphasized the study of Arabic language and culture. Support came from many institutions, including a committee comprised of the Lutheran Medical Center, the American-Arab Anti-Discrimination Committee, and the Arab-American Family Support Center. Its founding principal, Debbie Almontaser, strived to create a dual-language school based on what the community wanted. The school was slated to begin in 6th grade and continue through high school so that children could truly become bilingual and bicultural. [50]

As a religiously and politically diverse community, the group initially sought to offer instruction in both Hebrew and Arabic. However, this model proved to be too ambitious to implement, especially when taking into account all the various public education standards and regulations in New

York State. Eventually, the group decided to change its primary focus to an Arabic dual-language program that would foster values of inclusion and pluralism, while meeting local community needs. The school was also envisioned as a way to promote tolerance at a time of increased Islamophobia and racism.[51]

Defeat and the Lessons We Can Learn from It

Unfortunately, in the face of attacks from the press and several advocacy groups, the dual-language middle school program at Khalil Gibran International Academy did not survive. Although the Academy's mission was clear and well-structured, it became the target of much hostility—including a protest held outside New York's City Hall by a group called "Stop the Madrassa." Placard-waving crowds stood outside of the school for days, protesting the public school's Arab-English dual-language curriculum based on fears that it would indoctrinate children in radical Islamist ideology.

These reactions emanated from the post-9/11 context, which continued to plague New York City's Arab and Muslim institutions at the time. Despite what the New York Times described as an "organized movement to stop Muslim citizens who are seeking an expanded role in American public life,"[52] the Academy stood by its bilingual curriculum, as the program was already boasting strong academic and social results. However, in 2007 the city ceased to support the school and Principal Debbie Almontaser was forced to resign in the midst of a media scandal, despite the fact that she was a very well-known interfaith activist in New York City. A later case, brought before the Equal Employment Opportunity Commission, found that Almontaser was discriminated against by the New York City Department of Education. In a saddening personal and professional conclusion to Principal Almontaser's endeavor, the Khalil Gibran Academy was forced to abandon its dual-language program.

Today, by reinventing itself in a new school community, the Khalil Gibran International Academy carries forth Gibran's message of peace. It has transitioned from a middle school to a high school serving grades 9-12. Its mission is to:

> Develop, maintain, and graduate life-long learners who have a deep understanding of different cultural perspectives, a love of learning

and a desire for excellence with integrity. The school promotes holistic student development, and encourages them in their social, emotional, physical and intellectual growth. Along with our partners, we are dedicated to providing a supportive, student-centered, and collaborative learning environment where our students reach their full potential and grow into responsible global leaders who will impact the world around them.[53]

The school maintains English and Arabic language programs, though not in a dual-language context. While students who graduate from Khalil Gibran might not be fully proficient in Arabic, they still develop skills that build upon their own personal development and intercultural understanding and that will undeniably help them navigate future professional opportunities in sectors such as business and international relations.

Although the story of the Khalil Gibran Academy has a silver lining, Arabic-speaking populations remain a targeted and marginalized group. Fear of discrimination among Arab-Americans and Arabic-speaking communities in the United States has been high since 9/11. Arabic speakers are regularly portrayed in a negative light and are routinely viewed with suspicion, simply because of their linguistic background, ethnicity, or physical appearance.[54] Furthermore, this group tends to be categorically classified as Muslims when, in actuality, numerous Arabic speakers are Christians or come from other faith backgrounds. Misunderstandings and discriminatory attacks persist, and the heated and divided political climate in the United States of recent has not improved the situation. Overwhelmingly unfavorable attention has resulted in tension, uneasiness, and distress in the Arab-American community, as Zeena Zakharia, assistant professor of international and comparative education at the University of Massachusetts Boston, explains:

> I do think it is different for Arab communities, politically [...] People want to stay under the radar, they don't want to make trouble, they don't know if asking for things is asking for trouble.[55]

This sense of apprehension is palpable among those who speak Arabic in public, and even at home between parents and their children. Frequently, families prefer that their child not learn Arabic at all, as Zeena confirms:

> Arabic is not a high-status language. The politics around Arabic are difficult. Even in Lebanon, where I was the director of a dual-language school, I used to have parents who were coming back from the U.S. with their children to live in Lebanon saying, "I don't

want my child learning Arabic."[56]

This Arabic heritage language erosion that Zeena describes in the United States, and around the world, is unsettling. As we have seen in other linguistic communities, fear of discrimination and a strong desire to assimilate are incredibly powerful forces working against bilingualism in America. In the face of adversity, Arabic has become the latest victim in the long history of languages in the United States that have succumbed to mounting pressure based on social and ethnic prejudices.

Launching a Revival

Fortunately, parents and teaching professionals have achieved some success in combatting these stigmas, and Arabic language instruction in New York City has witnessed somewhat of a revival. In 2013, Carol Heeraman was approached by New York City's Office of English Language Learners about a project to create a dual-language program at her school, P.S./I.S. 30, in Brooklyn. She immediately had Arabic in mind to be the program's target language, since the majority of her school population spoke Arabic at home. Families from Yemen, Egypt, Lebanon, and Syria had recently started to move into the neighborhood, necessitating expanded Arabic bilingual offerings in public schools. The program was received with overwhelming enthusiasm from parents and was not a hard sell at all, as Arabic was already well-established in the school and in the community. Most importantly, the principal and staff did not have any negative preconceived notions about Arabic, and were well aware of its potential to prepare their students for success in the future.

Through the Arabic-English dual-language program, P.S./I.S. 30 quickly found a devoted partner in Qatar Foundation International, an organization dedicated to Arabic language and cultural education. Together, the school and the foundation worked to transform the dual-language initiative into a community effort.[57] Qatar Foundation International provided the necessary funding, curriculum planning, and materials to launch the bilingual program.[58] They lent legitimacy to the initiative, and happily shared their expertise in Arabic language education. The foundation also provided the funds to hire Mimi Met, an expert in language immersion, as a consultant to the program. In addition, school officials worked alongside the Arab-American Association—located nearby on Fifth Avenue in Brooklyn—

whose mission is "to support and empower the Arab immigrant and Arab-American community by providing services to help them adjust to their new home and become active members of society."[59] Linda Sarsour, the then-director of the Association and a well-known Palestinian-American political activist, was eager to get her own network involved to embrace and enhance the program. These partnerships allowed the Arabic dual-language program to gain access to both necessary funds and community support, two key components that contributed to their success.

In spite of the prejudice and stigmas that surround the Arabic-speaking community today, Arabic language skills are actually incredibly valued on a professional level, especially in the United States. In a post 9/11 context, many jobs now require Arabic, and there is an abundance of work opportunities related to the Arabic-speaking world. Most of the growth in Arabic language instruction in the U.S. has been at the university level, but it is a huge advantage for children to learn the language at an early age—highlighting the potential for impact that dual-language programs hold.[60]

Fluency in Arabic sets applicants apart from the competition for colleges, scholarships, and enrichment programs. Knowledge of Arabic, and familiarity with Arab culture, offers access to careers in business, diplomacy, journalism, security, and public policy, among many others.[61] Moreover, Arabic is one of the fastest growing second languages in the United States, with more than one million Americans speaking it at home.[62]

Principal Heeraman is quick to point out that many families interested in the Arabic dual-language program speak another language at home, such as Russian or Chinese, due to the multicultural landscape of the neighborhood the school serves. These families see the program as a form of academic enrichment, much like classes for "gifted" students that already exist in schools across the country. In this sense, Arabic language instruction is gaining the status it was so often denied in attempts past, as families now jump at the chance for their children to become fluent in a second, or even third, language.

Defining the Mission

In its development, the Arabic dual-language program encountered questions from parents and community members that necessitated a clear and defined scope of the program. For one, Arabic language instruction is often seen as beneficial to participation in Islamic religious tradition, most notably the reading of the Qur'an. Many parents initially expressed concern that the emphasis of the program would be more religious than linguistic, even though the instruction was taking place in a public school setting. To ensure a direct line of communication from the start, Principal Carol Heeraman made it very clear to parents that the school was not at all associated with any religious tradition, and that its mission was purely instructional and academic in nature. Its carefully-defined mission was to support the development of bilingual and biliterate students in English and in Arabic. This insistence on a clear mission helped the Arabic program move on from any lingering doubts or suspicions that negatively impacted the Arabic-English dual-language programs that came before.

After several months of extensive collaboration and planning, the Arabic dual-language program at P.S./I.S.30 opened its doors in September 2013. The dual-language curriculum was designed as a split day, where morning classes are taught in Arabic and afternoon classes in English, or vice versa. The school currently offers dual-language classes from Kindergarten to 3rd grade, adding a new grade every year as the original class moves up. As Principal Heeraman is also head of the middle school, I.S. 30, she plans to continue the Arabic dual-language curriculum all the way through 8th grade.

For all involved, the established importance of Arabic as an international and critical language has increased P.S./I.S. 30's popularity in the community, as Carol Heeraman confirms:

> For my parents who are knowledgeable and worldly, they are very receptive to it. They are banging down the doors to get their kids into the program. Next year, the hope is that we can open two Kindergarten classes instead of just one. And to continue all the way to 8th grade... I can't wait to graduate these babies who are now in 2nd grade. 8th graders who are bilingual and biliterate—it will be amazing. We'll have a whole graduation in Arabic. It's phenomenal. All of this is possible. [63]

This vision for the future created and carried out by Principal Heeraman is a true inspiration. Her leadership and zeal for Arabic dual-language programs in her community continue to touch the lives of the many children and families that pass through the program and are afforded the opportunity to learn and grow in two languages.

In spite of recent hardships and setbacks in the face of adversity, the New

York City Arabic-speaking community has achieved enormous success in establishing two bilingual programs in recent years. Much of their success lies in the unwavering support of school administrators, foundations, and local community organizations that allow for such valuable programs to exist in today's political climate. The Arabic dual-language story offers a much needed, and somewhat unexpected, complement to the story of the Bilingual Revolution. It vividly portrays the importance of collaboration and support from many different sources. Although active participants in their own dual-language program, Arabic-speaking parents were not, this time, the Dual-Language Program initiators. For the Arabic dual-language programs in New York City, it took a village to start their own Bilingual Revolution.

Chapter 8

Celebrating Culture: The Polish Community's Dual-Language Program

Greenpoint, in north Brooklyn, is home to the first Polish-English dual-language program in New York City. The program began at P.S. 34 in September 2015 with one Kindergarten class, and is set to expand each year with an additional incoming class. For nearly a century and a half, P.S. 34 has been a neighborhood institution in Greenpoint, an area known for its large Polish-American community, as indicated by its nickname, "Little Poland." The neighborhood boasts the second-largest concentration of Polish speakers in the United States after Chicago,[64] in part due to the large numbers of Poles who arrived in New York before the turn of the twentieth century.[65] Manhattan Avenue is at the heart of Little Poland, where one can find many Polish meat stores with strings of kielbasa, bakeries with Polish bread and babkas, and supermarkets with Polish pickles, jams, dried soups, and sauerkraut. With the addition of the Polish dual-language program, P.S. 34 has become a living link to Greenpoint's rich history and a symbol of the Bilingual Revolution in Brooklyn.

Launching a dual-language program in a culturally and historically Polish neighborhood in Brooklyn was an important milestone for both the Polish community and the city as a whole. When the program was formally inaugurated in 2015, parents, city and local officials, and diplomats were in attendance, as well as local Polish daily news stations that were on hand to cover the event.[66] District 14 Superintendent Alicja Winnicki, herself a Polish immigrant and a former principal of P.S. 34, congratulated Principal Carmen Asselta, teachers, and parents on the creation of the program in the heart of Greenpoint. Urszula Gacek, the Consul General of Poland in New York, praised the bilingual offerings of the school. Given her own personal background—Gacek is an English-born, Oxford-educated daughter of Polish immigrants who went on to become a Polish senator and a member of the European Parliament—Consul General Gacek explained, "I can't imagine not supporting the Polish dual-language program." The opening of the program was a moment of great pride for all involved—the culmination of the efforts of many dedicated parents, educators, and community actors.

The Strength of Collaboration

Carmen and Alicja credited the school's parents with the program's launch. The founding group started their initiative with a community survey to gauge interest in a Polish dual-language program back in 2014. Once they realized they had the numbers to build a strong case, they contacted Carmen and asked her to consider a dual-language program in Polish. Julia Kotowski recalls:

> The idea started with Polish mothers sitting in the park. Someone said that there's a law that allows for a dual-language program to be present in a school. A few of us got together, did some research, and wrote letters to Principal Asselta about our desire to start a program. That's when we met with Alicja Winnicki, the district superintendent, who presented our idea to the Department of Education.[67]

As stories told in many of the other chapters of this book demonstrate, many dual-language programs begin with grassroots campaigns led by parents. However, unique to the case of the Polish Dual-Language initiative in Greenpoint is the extraordinary support parents received from the district superintendent, along with P.S. 34's school administration and teaching staff. To ensure the success in their endeavor, school leaders promptly met with representatives from the Office of English Language Learners and presented the hard data parents had collected on the number of students in Greenpoint who qualified for bilingual services, as well as the number of interested families. The project was soon off to a running start, and, with the backing of the community and school system, quickly became a reality.

A Clearly-Defined Program

The dual-language program at P.S. 34 set out to provide English Language Learners and English-proficient students with an academically rigorous curriculum in both Polish and English. Elizabeth Czastkiewicz, a Polish language Kindergarten teacher in the dual-language program, explains the benefit of teaching Polish in a formal classroom setting to her student population:

> The children are all born here and the majority speak Polish at home. Those that have siblings tend to speak in English when they go home, but now parents are telling me that they go home and speak Polish. That was good to hear, that English is no longer their predominant language. They're much more confident now so that they can go home, they can demonstrate. At this age, Kindergarten and 1st grade, children want to demonstrate to their families and their parents, "Look at what I learned! This is what I'm learning!" Parents want that. Building that confidence so that they're not afraid to make a mistake is huge.[68]

This structure enables the students to build upon their academic skills in their first language and, eventually, transfer those skills to the second language. Students are expected to comprehend, speak, read, and write in both Polish and English upon the completion of the dual-language program in 5th grade. Through careful planning between teachers in both languages, students develop as bilingual, biliterate, and bicultural individuals.

Experiential and hands-on learning techniques are also integrated into the classroom through reading books aloud, songs, and arts and crafts, as well as through field trips and multicultural presentations outside the classroom. Carmen describes an example of such enrichment activities:

> The district took part in the Madlenka project, but every school developed their own projects according to the personality of their school or the mission of their teaching. The book celebrates multiculturalism; the book celebrates the richness of Madlenka's neighborhood. This little girl walks around the block to visit her neighbors, with each neighbor representing a different part of the world. My Kindergarten classes decided that they were going to build Madlenka's neighborhood in Greenpoint. This was the take of their grade: it's our neighborhood—celebrating the richness of the multicultural flavor of Greenpoint.[69]

For this project, children in the Polish dual-language class depicted bakeries, shops, homes adorned with Polish flags, and even pictures of revered Polish national figures. By celebrating the multicultural neighborhood they call home, the children developed a sense of pride in their own Polish culture.

That being said, even children who did not come from Polish heritage themselves were excited and thoroughly engaged in these kinds of cultural activities. These children also have much to gain from the Polish dual-language curriculum. Indeed, the program has witnessed a surge of families of non-Polish descent interested in the educational offerings for their children. Carmen describes the evolution of the program and its appeal to various parent groups:

> This Kindergarten class is very interesting because there are five families that are not of Polish descent at all, but who have opted into the Polish program. These families chose Polish simply because they want to expose their children to the language. Their children come in silent, not knowing one word. They want what I call a "productive struggle." When you come in not knowing and you struggle through it, but you come out achieving—that's a productive struggle. These families want that productive struggle for their children.[70]

The school now has an extensive waiting list for the Polish dual-language Kindergarten class. Despite the cap on admissions, some families have even been willing to put their child in the general program, in the hope that they could transfer into the dual-language program the next year. As is common with successful dual-language programs, demand has overrun supply, and schools are significantly limited by constraints on space and resources. The silver lining, of course, for the Polish dual-language program is that it has ample room to grow to better serve the needs of its expanding community.

The Multiple Ways to Preserve Heritage

In addition to the dual-language program, to preserve the linguistic and cultural identity of the Polish heritage community, Saturday and after-school programs are regularly offered. Historically, many Polish families in New York saw Saturday schools as a sufficient means of preserving their heritage, especially considering that they wanted their children to be completely immersed in English in the classroom. Alicja Winnicki, the district superintendent, explains:

> For a very long time, even when I was the principal of P.S. 34 where over 50 percent of students came from Polish-speaking homes, parents did not desire a dual-language program. They only wanted their kids to learn English as quickly as possible. The Polish community sent their children to public schools to learn English to

become successful here. The Polish heritage, the culture, the language... that was the role of the Saturday schools. The trend started reversing recently, with much younger families. These are young people who want their children to have an opportunity to be in a bilingual program and learn two languages simultaneously.[71]

This change in attitude quickly resulted in a new strategic outlook on Polish dual-language programs and Saturday enrichment programs, as well as how they can work together to better serve the Polish community. Julia Kotowski, one of the founding parents at P.S. 34, commented:

Saturday schools teach Polish culture and history. This is something that they're not going to have in the classroom to the same extent. It's something that we were taught in school back in Poland. It's not at all replacing the academic study of Polish, it's adding another level. It's another advantage of speaking both languages.[72]

Parents began to realize that Saturday schools were incredibly effective at maintaining ties to their heritage, but dual-language programs afforded their children the chance to master both English and Polish in a structured and continuous fashion. In this way, the two sets of Polish-English institutions complement each other by providing a comprehensive and highly rigorous cultural and linguistic curriculum for Polish families.

Positive Results

The Polish dual-language program has welcomed children of many different heritage backgrounds with open arms. For the diverse and robust New York Polish community, the dual-language program accommodates families of Polish heritage from recently arrived immigrants to second, third, or fourth generations looking to reconnect with their Polish roots. Carmen describes the makeup and achievement of her program in the following terms:

We have parents that are first-generation Poles, parents that were born here, and parents who immigrated when they were still babies and have no memory of living in Poland. We have children with Polish grandparents but were never taught Polish. They now have the opportunity to learn their heritage language, and they have the opportunity to do so in school.[73]

The ability of the dual-language program to connect generations of communities through education is one of its strongest and deeply personal characteristics. Through a renewed commitment to heritage language education in a dual-language program, relationships with family members once inaccessible or distant can deepen significantly. This opens up new realms of possibility for families, especially in immigrant communities, to preserve multi-generational bonds and connect their children to their customs, culture, and ancestry.

Through it all, the bonds of this close-knit Polish community have only been strengthened by the dual-language program. Vibrant community life, businesses, cultural centers, and cultural organizations such as Dobra Polska Szkoła, which has played a significant role in fostering the Polish bilingual revolution, have shown an outpouring of support for the bilingual endeavor and taken a vested interest in fostering the next generation of Polish-Americans. Alicja explains the bond she feels to her Polish heritage in the following terms:

> We have a strong sense of belonging and a strong connection with our history, our struggles as a nation and what kept us together. I frequent the Polish bookstore in Greenpoint all the time, just to keep in touch and immerse myself in literature, culture, and poetry. My daughter used to listen to her father reciting long poems from memory; she was exposed to these roots that really ground us in who we are. That's part of the heritage, and I know how strong it is in the Polish community. [74]

Alicja's moving testimony underscores the importance of the lived experience of heritage and culture. Tender moments lost in literature or even exchanging with family and friends play a role in how each family, child, and individual experiences their own culture.

The Greenpoint community is extremely fortunate to have managed to preserve and celebrate their Polish roots, and is an example for the rest of the country and world of how to nurture a multicultural way of life. The Polish dual-language program is a testament to the community's pride in its heritage and desire to pass its cultural and linguistic traditions on to the next generations of Polish-Americans. Thriving multicultural communities are excellent partners for dual-language education programs, who in turn produce highly competent bilingual and bicultural students. Together, neighborhood by neighborhood, these partnerships lay the groundwork for an enduring bilingual revolution that sustains precious linguistic heritages and enriches communities one school at a time.

Chapter 9

Paving the Way:
The Pioneers of Spanish
Dual-language Education

S panish is the second most common language spoken in New York City, with native Spanish speakers making up nearly a quarter of all New Yorkers. Consequently, many of the city's dual-language programs, both new and established, are in Spanish and English. Spanish programs have spread rapidly, often developing in neighborhoods with high numbers of English Language Learners. But the scope of Spanish dual-language programs reaches far beyond native Spanish speakers, enrolling students of varying backgrounds and abilities. The Spanish Bilingual Revolution was at the forefront of the Bilingual Revolution and today over 10,000 children attend Spanish dual-language programs in New York City. Much of the success of today's dual-language programs is thanks to the activism of those who worked to jumpstart Spanish bilingual programs in New York, as well as to the creativity and dedicated support of educators and administrators. Their story of embracing dual-language programs to better serve the Spanish-speaking community is both inspiring and motivating, and illustrates how far bilingual education has come over the recent decades.

How It All Began

It is tempting to think of dual-language programs as a creation of the recent past, but the promise of bilingualism, biliteracy, and biculturalism that is central to today's dual-language programs greatly resembles what early Puerto Rican activists and educators in the 1960s hoped for when campaigning for the first bilingual programs. Ofelia Garcia explains:

> Dual-language, if done well, is precisely what the Puerto Rican

community would have wanted for their children back in the beginning. These parents were demanding an education that was truly bilingual, no matter what the linguistic characteristics were.[75]

However, even though these early activists desired bilingual Spanish-English programs that would allow their children to grow in both languages, that was not what they originally got. This is because the story of bilingual education in New York and in the United States is complicated by political and social battles that translated into varying outcomes in the classroom. The debate on what bilingual education is or should be is ongoing and frequently becomes intertwined with heated discussions on immigration and assimilation in the United States. Garcia describes the underlying tensions at this earlier time and its impact on Spanish bilingual education:

Bilingual education in those days was in a different place. The city was mostly Puerto Rican at the time. They were all Spanish-speaking and it was very political. These pioneers wanted a bilingual program that would take care of the whole bilingual continuum of the community, not just those who did not know English. The programs implemented soon became irrelevant, because the community became fully English-speaking and therefore did not qualify. Since the beginning, there has been a tension between what communities wanted, what school authorities were willing to give them, and then, once this whole dual-language movement started, the realization that they were being left out.[76]

Instead of dual-language classrooms that build upon fluencies in both English and Spanish, the bilingual programs offered to Spanish speakers from the outset were largely intended to promote monolingualism and the mastery of English. These programs were only offered to students who lacked proficiency in English and utilized Spanish only as a tool to teach English, thereby cutting off access to many Spanish heritage students who were born in the United States and who came in with an existing knowledge of the English language.

But the tide began to change in the field of bilingual education. Research began to be published that pointed to the benefits of bilingual education when taught in two languages. Bilingual activists rose to positions of power within school districts and administrations in New York City, elevating bilingual issues to the top of the agenda. Carmen Dinos, a retired professor of education and a pioneer in the field of bilingual education, succeeded in creating New York's first bilingual public school programs in the 1960s and 1970s. She explains her experience at this turning point in the history of bilingual education:

> Towards the end of the Civil Rights movement, the Bilingual Office was developed as a division of the Board of Education, with Hernan LaFontaine—the former principal of P.S. 25 in the Bronx, the first bilingual school—as the director. They were dealing with the whole city at the policy level. That's when I understood that education is so tightly connected with politics. The field bloomed at the same time; more and more researchers in Canada were proving the benefits of bilingual education. Suddenly, this was not a whim. There was solid proof that it was good for kids.[77]

School administrators also began to pick up on the "dual-language" trend sweeping the nation, cleverly hiding the loaded term "bilingual," which had taken on a negative context. Ofelia Garcia describes one founding principal's logic and strategy to implement a similar program at his school:

> Back then, there were a few luminaries. One was Sid Morrison, the principal of P.S. 84. Much to his credit, in the mid-1980s, Sid started saying, "What we have doesn't work. The community has changed; it is no longer Spanish-monolingual it is gentrifying quickly. We have to have a program for whoever wants to join." To distance itself from the transitional bilingual programs, he picked up this label of "dual-language," which was beginning to gain traction in the country.[78]

This strategy worked. With the help of committed educators, administrators, and parents, Spanish dual-language programs took off in New York City. As of this writing, 45 schools serving more than 10,000 students across the city host Spanish dual-language programs from Kindergarten to high school.

Former Department of Education Chancellor Carmen Fariña's administration put an unprecedented focus on developing bilingual education programs. Deputy Chancellor Milady Baez describes the philosophy of the Department in regard to bilingual education as the following:

> We understand that bilingual education has a history in the United States. It has not been always a very positive one. There have been many groups of people who have had to fight, to struggle. We have had to convince parents that their children needed to be educated in

more than one language. We know that children have the potential; they have the ability to transfer their knowledge from one language to the other. We know that when our students speak more than one language, they are higher achievers than students who only speak one language.[79]

This kind of all-encompassing support for bilingual education at the highest administrative level is overwhelmingly powerful, as these leaders hold the keys to the creation of scores of dual-language programs.

Milady, herself a native Spanish speaker, also has a deep personal connection to the field of bilingual education. From not being able to understand the language of instruction in the classroom as a young and recently-arrived immigrant to United States, Milady Baez went on to become a New York City bilingual teacher and later a school principal in Jackson Heights, Queens. There, Milady was able to create what she called her "dream school" where she opened dual-language and bilingual enrichment programs in Spanish so that, in her words, "every student and family was afforded the opportunity to access the program of instruction they so desired."

Currently, as Deputy Chancellor in the Department of Education, Milady is at the helm of the management and creation of programs for English Language Learners. She constantly encourages parents to fight for their right to bilingual education programs in public schools. To achieve their goals, sometimes all it takes is to ask, as Milady confirms:

Parents are powerful in our educational system. Many parents do not know that if they unite and that if they ask for these programs, principals have the responsibility of making it happen in their schools.[80]

Powerful alliances that are formed with educators and administrators like Milady often start with parent grassroots movements and a simple ask. Milady's warm and receptive welcome of dual-language programs and bilingual opportunities for students of varying linguistic backgrounds, and her commitment to serving her student population in a way that fits their needs and goals, is an outstanding example of the positive role administrators can play in the Bilingual Revolution.

Some Shining Examples

One of the myriad of Spanish dual-language programs that exist today in New York City is at P.S. 133 in Brooklyn. There, the first Spanish-English dual-language Kindergarten class opened in 2012. As the Spanish-speaking world is rich in diversity, children who participate in the program at P.S. 133 tap into the long history and relationship between the Hispanic community and the City of New York. Following a 50/50 model, half of the students are English-speaking and half Spanish-speaking, with half the daily instruction for all subjects in Spanish and the other half in English. Last year, P.S. 133, along with fourteen other schools in New York City, was designated a Model Dual-language Program by former Department of Education Chancellor Carmen Fariña.[81]

The Amistad Dual Language School was founded by a group of teachers and parents led by Elia Castro, a bilingual educator, with the support of Lydia Bassett, the former principal of the W. Hayward Burns School, and New Visions for Public Schools, a nonprofit that works to revitalize and improve New York City public schools. Amistad opened in Northern Manhattan in 1996 and provides its students in Washington Heights, Hamilton Heights, and Inwood with a Spanish-English dual-language curriculum for both English- and Spanish-dominant students.

The underlying principle of instruction at Amistad is that children acquire a second language in the same way they acquire their first. Teachers utilize many English as a Second Language (ESL) strategies for teaching Spanish as a Second Language, proven to be effective regardless of the child's native language. The school embraces a multidisciplinary instructional approach by offering a comprehensive program in music, dance, and visual and theater arts in addition to more customary standard academic subjects. Through their experiential and project-based learning approach, Amistad nurtures creativity and cultivates intellectual curiosity in its students—all while achieving language proficiency and attaining a high standard of academic success. The school's mission statement embodies their unique approach to dual-language education:

> The Amistad Dual Language School is a community of learners that embraces the unique path of each individual. Together we foster a sense of communal responsibility and solidarity through the celebration of culture, language, and diversity. Our children will

move forward, ready to meet the academic and the social demands of the larger community, taking with them the magic of discovery and the power of two languages. Our language allocation policy varies by grade to accommodate both conversational and academic language acquisition. [82]

Amistad has been rated a Five Star school by Great Schools, a nationwide online source of school performance rankings and information. The school's proven track record of success in graduating bilingual students is the primary reason why it is so attractive to families. According to Miriam Pedraja, Amistad's former school principal, by 3rd grade approximately 70 percent of Spanish-dominant language students who enrolled in the school in Kindergarten had become equally proficient in English and Spanish. [83]

Cypress Hills Community School in Brooklyn takes a different approach. It offers a hybrid Spanish dual-language program in both a school and community center environment. In 1997, with support from New Visions for Public Schools, the school was founded by parents and the Cypress Hills Local Development Corporation. Strong parent leadership is a hallmark of the school, as evidenced by the fact that Maria Jaya, a parent herself, currently acts as a co-principal. She recalls how she and other parents fought for their children's education:

> The revolution started thirty years ago, only to have the [original] program open ten years later. Our children were in a so-called "bilingual" program, but the programs were not well designed or well prepared. Some teachers did not have the right licenses. Parents didn't have the right information. The way that I signed students up for the bilingual program was not based on their needs, but based on if they had a Latino-sounding name. Parent meetings were all in English, so we requested a translator. Finally, they started translating but they sent those who requested translation services to the corners of the room. This put a huge responsibility on the person translating and parents struggled to give feedback, segregated in one corner. That was our first fight: we wanted to participate and we wanted to be part of our children's education, but we didn't have an equal opportunity to do so. Soon, the teachers noticed this group of parents that really wanted change, and they started giving us information.[84]

The Cypress Hills story echoes the struggles that Spanish bilingual education faced throughout New York City as parents advocated for dual-language programs that empowered their communities in both languages. It took persistence and a lot of courage to demand the services and programs that they wanted and deserved, especially after years of program offerings that did not meet the expectations of the Spanish-speaking community.

But the obstacles Cypress Hills faced were not only limited to the classroom or parent gatherings. Throughout its first thirteen years of existence, the Cypress Hills Community School operated within other school buildings and without a permanent campus. Cypress Hills had no access to a gym, lacked its own library and auditorium, and suffered from major classroom overcrowding—with many sections conducted in aging portable classrooms. In 2010, the school moved into a brand-new building, the result of years of tremendously hard work on the part of parents, students, and the Cypress Hills community, as well as the advocacy efforts of elected officials. Ultimately, the support of the City Council, Department of Education, and the School Construction Authority was critical in creating a space that reflected the input of students, parents, and teachers. The result of true dedication and tireless efforts, the school now has programmatically-appropriate, thoughtfully-designed classrooms with up-to-date technology, a greenhouse, a science lab, a sizable and well-stocked library, spaces dedicated to the arts, a café-style cafeteria, and a multipurpose gym.[85]

The school continues to blossom as it provides educational opportunities for bilingual enrichment through many avenues. The Cypress Hills Learning Center offers an extended school day during the week in order to provide innovative enrichment and differentiated instruction in art, dance, music, sports, conflict-resolution, and academic support. The school also partners with organizations such as Young Audiences New York and the Brooklyn Queens Conservatory of Music. The programs and initiatives of Cypress Hills provide an exemplary model for others interested in creating their own bilingual enrichment programs.

These Spanish dual-language programs serve as a source of inspiration for future pioneers in bilingual education to push the limits and create opportunities for children in their communities to become bilingual or maintain their bilingualism. From their inception, they have paved the way for bilingual programs in the United States and have constantly been at the forefront of the evolution and progression of bilingual education. Without the determination, commitment, and inspiration of parent and educator pioneers who fought for the right to develop bilingual programs that educate the whole child, there would not be a Bilingual Revolution today.

Chapter 10

High Achievers:
The High School for Dual Language &
Asian Studies

A s dual-language parents and educators scramble for ways to improve their schools, meet students' needs, and push back against a test-score-driven educational culture, many in the field may wonder what the right path might look like. Often, dual-language programs grow organically and without much uniformity, essentially "reinventing the wheel" with the formation of each new program. Knowing this, it is essential to promote knowledge sharing, create standards, provide resources and curriculum materials, and ensure that teaching practices are consistent with those of successful dual-language programs. To continue the Bilingual Revolution and cut back on the significant workload that inherently comes with the implementation of new kinds of educational offerings, it is equally important to learn from pioneer schools that have already developed their own resources and forge a path to success.

An Exemplary Model

The High School for Dual Language and Asian Studies stands out as an example from which much can be learned. Founded in 2003, the school is a highly competitive institution with a student population of both native English and Mandarin speakers. Located in downtown Manhattan on the fifth floor of an old school building, the school serves over 400 students who come from families who speak English, Spanish, Bengali, and a combination of Chinese dialects, including Mandarin, Cantonese, Taosonese, Fuzhonese, Shanghainese, and Wenzounese. The high school has consistently demonstrated excellence in English and mathematics, among other subjects. Despite its relatively high proportion of economically-

79

disadvantaged children, the school continues to place competitively in national and state rankings, as evaluated by students' performance on state-mandated tests and college-readiness.[86] As defined within its mission statement, the school is:

> Devoted to providing quality instruction and guidance counseling to promote the academic and social development of our students as well as their linguistic capacity, cultural appreciation, and international and global awareness.[87]

More importantly, as the vast majority of dual-language programs in the United States abruptly end after 5th grade, this school occupies a unique position as one of the rare public high schools in the United States that offers a dual-language program.

The High School for Dual Language and Asian Studies is among the schools featured in "Schools to Learn From," a noteworthy study undertaken by Stanford University with the support of the Carnegie Corporation of New York. In their case study, the authors did an in-depth analysis of the dual-language program in order to understand why this school in particular succeeded exceptionally well in preparing its students for college and future careers. In their interviews with the school's students, parents, and educators, the researchers highlighted the school community's "relentless commitment to serve students and a focus on their strengths and needs."[88]

The praises sung by these authors lend legitimacy to the steadfast efforts of the school community to establish itself as a force to be reckoned with in bilingual education. Their tireless work ethic and constant drive to achieve success have propelled the school to the national and international stage, a testament to their efforts.

The Birth of a Unique Program

Ron Woo, a professor of education law and a program consultant at the NYU Metropolitan Center for Research on Equity and the Transformation of Schools, spearheaded the development of the High School for Dual Language and Asian Studies under the leadership of then-Chancellor of the Department of Education, Joel Klein. Ron recalls:

> In 2003, the Chancellor asked me to help him put together an innovative program. I suggested a dual-language high school at the

former Seward Park High School, a large school that was not performing well. This was at the beginning of the Bloomberg administration, when they were closing down underperforming schools. The problem was they made small schools, but forgot to create a small school for the large number of Chinese immigrants at Seward Park. We got together and said, "Why not try a dual-language Chinese program? It would be a catch for the Chinese immigrant population, and there would be others coming in who would learn Chinese as a foreign language.[89]

The school proposal for Chinese immigrant students received the full support of the Chancellor and was the first of its kind in the nation. The founding team was tasked with identifying resources for the school's creation and met with the China Institute of America[90] and the Asia Society[91] in New York City, which assisted with curriculum development. The team also recruited Li Yan, the current principal, who turned their concept paper into what is now the High School for Dual Language and Asian Studies.

The school is at the forefront of the field of secondary dual-language education. These types of high schools offer a college preparatory curriculum and provide a much-needed multilingual continuation for existing dual-language programs in elementary and middle schools. As the High School for Dual Language and Asian Studies is now well-established and highly successful, few people remember how difficult it was to convince families to join the program when the school first opened its doors. Principal Li Yan recalls:

> People need to get used to the idea of new schools. Parents used to say, "Your school is new! Why am I sending the kids here? You have nothing to show me here." I ran into a lot of problems with parents refusing to send their kids to us. It was very difficult for the first three or four years because people were looking for results and I had nothing to show them. It's a convincing game. Anything we did at school, any progress the school made—we made sure the parents knew. We actually asked each student to give a personal presentation of their work, and that won a lot of parents over. Four years after the first graduating class, we started building our reputation.[92]

It is revealing to look back and see how far the school has come. Principal Li Yan's comments point to a very important phenomenon that plays against the creation of bilingual programs: the fear of the unknown. This becomes even more apparent as students get older, especially at the high school level, and families become more and more concerned about choosing the right school to prepare their students for the competitive college application process. However, with every dual-language school success story, this fear diminishes as parents become more knowledgeable of the many benefits of a bilingual education. As proven by Yan, her colleagues, her students, and her families, the High School for Dual Language and Asian Studies is nothing if not a success.

A Cultural and Linguistic Curriculum

Unlike other cities, high school selection in New York is an open choice process whereby each middle school student may choose up to twelve schools from a list provided by the Department of Education. To be accepted by the High School for Dual Language and Asian Studies, students need not speak both Chinese and English because of the school's two tracks: one for English speakers and one for Chinese speakers. As a result, some students begin their language immersion at a very late age. Professor Ron Woo describes the ambitious goals of the program as the following:

> The model was built on the notion that by the time they'd finished, they would be fully bilingual. Those who started with no Chinese would catch up over the four-year period. The Chinese speakers were already bilingual, or would be catching up on their English because they were immigrant students. By the time they got to their second year, you might see them co-existing in the same classes. There is a spectrum of language levels, which creates some tension, but at least there is something there.[93]

As Professor Woo points out, this speedy transition throughout high school from monolingualism to bilingualism is a noble, albeit sometimes demanding, goal. Affording high school students the opportunity to start and become fluent in a second language at the high school level, as is possible at the High School for Dual Language and Asian Studies, is an incredible achievement.

The educational backgrounds of both Chinese-speaking and English-speaking students at the school vary widely. Some Chinese-speaking students were born in China and attended elementary and middle school there before moving to the United States to complete their education at the high school level. Others were born in the United States, relocated to China during their childhood, and returned to the United States to complete their high school careers. Students who are English-proficient vary in their linguistic backgrounds and Chinese abilities, and a number of them are former English Language Learners. The school also serves students whose primary language is English and have no Chinese proficiency prior to coming to the school. This group is drawn to the program because of their interest in the Chinese language and culture, as well as the school's focus on biliteracy.

The High School for Dual Language and Asian Studies offers students a multifaceted curriculum. In addition to their other subjects, all students take four years of Mandarin, either in the form of a native language arts class or Chinese as a second language. Native English-speakers attend a double period of Chinese every day to ensure that they are prepared to pass the required Chinese Regents and Advanced Placement (AP) Chinese exams, in addition to the five other exams a student must pass to qualify for a New York State Regents diploma with honors. Teachers work alongside guidance counselors and parent coordinators to help students select their courses and lend additional support to students who need it.

Most of the students at the high school come from recently-arrived immigrant families that have been in the United States for less than ten years. These learners require additional services to ensure their academic success due to language barriers and the added challenge of adapting to a new culture. To assist these students and their families in overcoming these obstacles, all written materials are provided in English, Chinese, Bengali, and Spanish. Staff members also go the extra mile when they can, as the principal, school secretary, guidance counselor, and several teachers are all bilingual and able to translate any materials the school provides that are not written in both languages.

The school also provides an enriched high school experience, emphasizing a rigorous academic curriculum for students from diverse cultural and socioeconomic backgrounds in both English and Chinese. Thalia Baeza Milan, a current junior at the school, already spoke English and Spanish when she arrived in the United States three years ago from Guyana, and was eager to take advantage of the opportunity at the High School for Dual Language and Asian Studies to learn Chinese. She describes her time at the high school in these terms:

The experience has helped me appreciate different cultures and work through difficulties—like mixing up the words for "fried chicken" and "acrobat." I know the steps to overcoming challenges and the steps to being comfortable in an environment I've never been in before. That's something that will be helpful.[94]

Thalia points to the productive "struggle" of language learning that many bilingual children grow to appreciate and value. This process, although challenging and humorous at times—as Thalia points to in her language mix up—generates deeper learning, builds authentic engagement, and emphasizes the various building blocks of comprehension that are applicable to so many skills in life.

In addition, the school introduces students to a variety of Asian cultures, with a primary focus on China. When students are not engaged in the rigorous academic program, they can participate in clubs ranging from film and computer science to varsity sports such as badminton and wrestling. In preparation for university, students also have plenty of opportunities to earn college credit, tour campuses, and compete for scholarships.

Some students even participate in a Saturday school program at the high school, utilized for instructional work. The program includes physical education and additional English as a Second Language classes and serves approximately 150 kids each week.[95] It also affords students a community space to complete homework or projects, as they may not have the space or environment to work productively at home. This approach has proven to be very efficient in increasing students' academic performance and overall engagement with the school.

Long-term Impact

For the Bilingual Revolution at large, the story of the High School for Dual Language and Asian Studies is insightful. Imagine the realm of opportunities that would spring from dual-language high schools, continuing the incredible accomplishments of existing dual-language elementary and middle school programs that serve populations of fully bilingual students. The sky is the limit for these high school programs, and the High School for Dual Language and Asian studies is just the beginning.

There is no reason why the Bilingual Revolution should stop in primary schools. In fact, by embracing secondary education dual-language programs, we afford our children the opportunity to become highly successful multilingual individuals, prepared to enter the academic and professional arenas with the tools they need to succeed. The story of the High School for Dual Language and Asian Studies is a story of unparalleled success that can be replicated in high schools across the country and the world. The Bilingual Revolution has the power to touch children's lives through adolescence, young adulthood, and beyond. It is up to us to provide them the opportunity to do so.

Chapter 11

The Roadmap to Creating Your Own
Dual-Language Program

The following chapter presents a roadmap for parents interested in creating a dual-language program in a public school. The central theme of this roadmap and of this book is that parents can make a difference in their communities by starting dual-language programs, no matter where they are located. These programs can improve schools and empower communities in unprecedented ways thanks to the efforts of parent groups. The information presented in the following pages will help parents organize themselves, build a strong proposal, and inspire others to join their initiatives along the way.

The roadmap is a suggested path for both parents and educators to use as a guide. It details how to put together information sessions, organize volunteer groups, prepare a convincing rationale for principals and teachers, develop strategies to canvass the community, identify potential families who are interested in enrolling their children in the dual-language program, and work efficiently with all stakeholders to get the project off the ground. An abridged roadmap can also be found in the appendix and downloaded from this book's official website.[96] The suggestions and strategies offered in this book are by no means exhaustive as it is impossible to take into account the many differences that separate school districts and linguistic communities. Therefore, parents are encouraged to create their own map, making the necessary adjustments to fit their community's needs. The original roadmap, which inspired this book, was written by parents for parents almost ten years ago to share their successful approach in the hopes that others would follow and implement their own dual-language programs in public schools.[97] Many parent groups and initiatives inspired by the original roadmap are featured in the case studies presented in this book.

The roadmap is divided into three phases: Phase One introduces ways to create a core of interested families (a family base) through community outreach and organizing committees; Phase Two shares strategies to develop a strong rationale for a dual-language program and to present it to a potential school site; and Phase Three focuses on the implementation and planning a dual-language program so that it will succeed from the first day of school.

Phase One: Reaching Out to the Community

Creating a Base of Interested Families

Forming a base of interested families is the first step in the process of creating a dual-language program. As a parent-led grassroots undertaking, it is critically important that you develop a strong group of families that will seriously consider not only enrolling their children in a dual-language program but will also support the initiative as it travels through all of the ups and downs of starting a new educational endeavor. From now on, you can consider yourself an entrepreneur with a passion for multilingualism, a commitment to public education, and a willingness to connect with dozens, if not hundreds, of individuals in your community to form this base.

If you are initiating this endeavor with a target language already in mind, your next step will be to find parents who share this common interest. You can start by forming a core group of parents you know and trust. These are parents who will take part in your shared vision even if they do not have children who will benefit from this initiative. A good example of the effectiveness of a "core group" is the Japanese Dual-Language Program initiative presented in Chapter Two, which illustrates the importance of the commitment and expertise of parents.

Parents who follow this roadmap generally expect a brand new dual-language program to run from pre-Kindergarten or Kindergarten through 5th grade. This time span will vary depending upon the resources of your individual school, as well as how grade levels are organized in your school district. Some parents have more long-term goals and try to plan for their initiative to continue through middle school or even high school. Indeed, it is important to feel that these programs have the potential to grow and expand naturally into middle and high school programs, as demonstrated by the Spanish, Chinese, and French dual-language programs presented earlier.

If you are not initiating this endeavor with a target language already in mind but are interested in dual-language education as a way to educate your child, it is preferable to research your community's linguistic heritage in order to gauge the support you might receive. Understanding the cultural nuances with which a specific community will judge your proposal will be key, and identifying partners and fellow educational entrepreneurs from within the target culture will help to facilitate your project by presenting it in a way that is typically acceptable or preferred by a community. The Japanese initiative described in Chapter Two, for instance, relied upon five mothers, two of whom were Japanese and served as liaisons with the Japanese community. Their understanding of the cultural norms and customs of the community from which they were trying to recruit families helped them make important strategic choices. This was particularly true for the school administrators and other members of the initiative who did not speak Japanese or have an extensive knowledge of Japanese culture.

The Japanese group understood that there is a real need for bicultural understanding when you present a program and offer a service. They communicated with interested families in both Japanese and English. They took the time to explain the American educational system and its advantages to newly-arrived Japanese parents, as well as the similarities and differences when compared with the system of education in Japan. Throughout all their exchanges, they tried to answer all questions in an open and honest manner. The fact that the group was able to consult everyone and bring in their points of view to the discussion spoke volumes about their determination to be inclusive and respectful of all members' cultural backgrounds. In this particular case, cultural sensitivity was key to the success of the project's recruiting and implementation phases.

As a parent, you can also reach out to your own community by announcing publicly—through social media, community blogs, signs in public places, or word of mouth—that you are looking for people who are interested in helping create a dual-language program in a specific language. There are many advantages to basing your initiative upon a particular linguistic community. A large group of potentially interested parents may already exist and a community network of businesses, religious centers, community centers, and children who are native speakers of another language may be present within the boundaries of your school district. This was the case with the Arabic, Polish, and Italian dual-language programs presented in the previous chapters.

Once your group has gathered enough volunteers, you can start organizing committees to divide up the various tasks. Several committees can be organized including, but not limited to: a community outreach committee, a school location committee, and a curriculum support committee. Additional committees can also be included at various stages of the process based on the initiative's urgent needs, i.e. a teacher recruitment committee, a fundraising committee, or an after-school program committee, to name just a few. Again, these are suggestions and it is up to you to adjust this model to your local reality and the number of people interested in this initiative.

Collecting Data

Your community outreach committee should focus on identifying potential students and gathering family data. This will help you to get the word out so that a critical mass of people hears about the initiative and decides to sign their children up as potential candidates for the dual-language program. You should try to collect data on:

- The number of families interested in the program,
- The languages spoken at home and understood by the children,
- Children's dates of birth and their anticipated entry into primary school,
- Families' school district or school zone.

These are essential first steps in identifying candidates for the dual-language program. This data collection will also help you determine whether the dual-language program you support will be one-way (with native speakers of one language receiving instruction in an additional language) or two-way (with native speakers of both languages present in the classroom, frequently split half and half in ratio). This decision will be based upon the number of native speakers that you will enroll.

It is imperative to identify enough students for the opening class to be created. To set a target number, you will need to verify several things. First, you must research:

- The average number of children enrolled in an entering grade in your school district, as the number may vary from place to place and even from grade to grade. For example, there might be a class size difference between pre-Kindergarten and Kindergarten, or between classes in elementary school and classes in secondary school (middle school, junior high school, etc.).

- Additionally, you should look into the mandate under which a school district operates with regard to non-native speakers of the national or official language. In the case of New York City[98] and New York State, the law requires that schools offer a dual-language or transitional bilingual program if there are at least twenty children in the district whose native or home language is not English.[99] They are then categorized as English Language Learners (ELLs) or English as a New Language (ENLs).

If your school district operates under similar mandates that may bring extra support to your initiative, your research will need to:

- Determine the number of children by school district or zone considered non-native speakers or learners of English (or official language). These children will need to speak the same mother tongue to be in the same dual-language classroom.
- Determine the number of children by school district or zone considered bilingual (in this case, children who already know both English and the target language at various levels).
- Determine the number of children by school district or zone considered native speakers of the national or official language (in this case, English) who have no knowledge of the target language but whose families are committed to dual-language education in the target language that you have set.

This data will help you explain how your dual-language program will serve different needs. Doing so may also help you secure additional funding from state agencies or philanthropic organizations, particularly those that support English Language Learners. These statistics can also be powerful tools to craft a rationale that will convince principals of the need for such a program.

Identifying Families

Frequently, potential enrollment will start off with a large base and end up with a small group on opening day. For your specific initiative, it is advisable that you recruit more students than are necessary to open a bilingual program in your local schools. Since schools may have a minimum class number for a program to be viable—although it may be possible for some school principals to have a certain degree of discretion as to what the minimum number of students should be—this will demonstrate to your school principal, superintendent, or school board that there is a large enough pool of potential students for a bilingual program. This approach will also compensate for the loss of families that initially showed interest but decided to drop out of the program, move out of the district, or change schools.

It is very likely that you will receive interest and data for children with different years of birth—even children not yet born—in which case you will need to prepare a spreadsheet of birth dates and base your strategy on the number of potential candidates per year. Often, school calendars and school application deadlines will dictate the timing and strategy upon which to establish your initiative successfully.

There are multiple ways of finding, identifying, and recruiting interested families. You can do this through an announcement, letter, flyer, or poster that you can distribute when you attend meetings or give presentations.[100] It is important to take into account that starting a new dual-language program in your district is a long process. You should try to identify families with children young enough to be candidates for the program when the program will actually start. In some cases, this identification process should be done as early as one to two years before the program is launched. Cases in which, for a variety of reasons, founding parents were unable to get their children in the program, despite having put in all the work are discussed in previous chapters, and are a very unfortunate reality especially when working on a rushed timeline.

Because most bilingual programs in U.S. public schools start either in pre-Kindergarten, when children are four-years old, or Kindergarten, when children are five-years old, identifying children means reaching out to local preschools and daycare centers, private schools, language schools, cultural centers, religious institutions, parent associations, Head-Start programs, and city agencies that support families, among many others.[101] You can also engage in conversations with parents at local playgrounds, in stores, at supermarkets, and in schools where families might be looking for options for younger siblings. Identifying potential families that are already in a school also means that they could have connections to the school principal or parent coordinator, and can provide valuable insights into the school's administration.

Many of the program initiators interviewed for this book demonstrated great creativity. Some wore clothes, hats, or badges that piqued other parents' curiosity. They created web pages and used social media to centralize sign-up forms and to disseminate information and updates on the initiative. They reached out to local newspapers, community blogs, and parenting blogs so that families outside of their inner circles could find out about the project. They informed owners of local businesses and posted signs, particularly if these businesses were identifiable as centralized locations for speakers or proponents of the target language or cultural group. Some of the French Dual-Language Program initiators, for instance, put flyers up in playgrounds and grocery stores where they knew there would be French speakers. They also visited churches with large Francophone populations and approached people on the street or on the subway if they heard them speaking French. They reached out to all the French-speaking media outlets that they could find and called in to Francophone radio shows. They created a centralized email address and fielded hundreds of requests from parents. They spent hours and hours of their time on the initiative, lending advice to other parents about topics such as the school registration process or the difference between starting in Kindergarten versus pre-K, among many other things. The work of these parents was remarkable and they deserve our congratulations as their actions served more than just their own interests, extending far beyond their circle of family and friends for years to come. These dual-language programs initiators were true agents of change.

Community Outreach

A critically important task to undertake early in your effort is to create a community support base, which could include influential individuals, elected officials, and supportive organizations. This involves attending community meetings and informing the public about the Dual-Language Program initiative. Key local players to contact and meet may vary from place to place, but the support that you receive from them is not to be underestimated. It can be informative and useful for you to book an appointment with school officials (including the State Department of Education, District Superintendent, Office of Language Learners, etc.). These officials will probably have questions and it is imperative that you are well prepared to answer. Parents can meet with these officials before meeting with principals if they wish to gain insight on the local budget or garner some political support. However, it is important to include school principals in these exchanges as well as to assess their own understanding of dual-language education. This is particularly important after you have collected enough data to convince a principal of the need for a dual-language program in his or her district. The next section will take a closer look at some of the rationales that can convince them.

You may find it very useful to exchange information with parent associations, parent coordinators, and teachers, as they can share valuable insights about a school's climate and openness to new ideas. In addition, reaching out to community education councils, school boards, community boards, and local council members is important as they can help push your initiative over bureaucratic hurdles or lend assistance when you hit a roadblock. Your community outreach committee can also organize small gatherings at home, or in public spaces such as local coffee shops, restaurants or bakeries to pitch your ideas, gauge interest, or recruit potential families. In the case of such a gathering, you can invite one or all of the above-mentioned stakeholders to give a speech or share remarks.

Finally, the language that you have selected for your dual-language program is connected to a larger network of national and international supporters and institutions that can also provide important resources and assistance. This network includes embassies, consulates, honorary consuls, cultural centers serving a language or a country, foundations with a focus on education or community development, tourism offices, international or U.S. chambers of commerce that serve businesses from two or more countries, as well as heritage and cultural societies and federations. These are important partners to join forces with. They will often value your vision and drive your endeavor because it has the potential to generate fruitful ventures and open new markets for them.

Curriculum Support

Your curriculum support committee can provide assistance at various stages during the process. First, they can focus on compiling and sharing information about the many cognitive, academic, personal, and professional benefits of dual-language education during information sessions with parents in the community. It can also organize site visits to existing dual-language programs to determine best practices and to see first-hand how a program is administered. Interactions with established dual-language programs are an excellent way to ask questions about parental involvement and loyalty to the program, program sustainability, fundraising efforts, and needs in terms of resources, teachers, and administrative support. Often, principals and teachers of schools with existing dual-language programs are happy to share their insights with their counterparts who are researching the possibility of establishing a similar program. By learning about the successes and failures of these schools, you will be able to create a better program for your own initiative. The group should see that each visit is well-documented and that its observations and information are shared at committee meetings. Finally, the committee should meet with and invite parents who have succeeded in creating a dual-language program to learn from their experiences.

Phase 2: Developing a Convincing Rationale and Locating a Host School

At the end of their collaborative work, the various committees must be prepared to present the collected data to a principal and a school community. Before approaching a school principal with your idea, it is advisable to build a persuasive argument that will help you convince him or her, as well as other administrators involved, of the importance of your proposal. It can be very difficult to sell a French, Japanese, or Russian dual-language program, for example, to a school that is already very successful or oversubscribed. Parents should therefore develop a list of arguments that speak to the advantages of creating such a program in a public school, especially if that school is currently underperforming. It may be useful to base your argument on the school leader's own personal motivations. For instance, a new principal might be seeking recognition and a dual-language program would be a concrete way to leave their mark on the school, and even the community. A successful bilingual program can bring a lot of positive visibility to a school, advance its reputation, and attract new sources of funding. Additional families brought in by the dual-language program may also be more willing to fundraise to help the school succeed.

The convincing arguments are many. A critical number of non-native language learners need dual-language instruction in order to learn to speak English. Dual-language programs impart a lifelong gift of a second language to all children in the community. For second- or third-generation immigrant community families, dual-language programs safeguard their language and cultural heritage and enable them to share these with all children. A dual-language program will also continue to benefit the entire school community as new, highly motivated families join the school each year. These parents bring with them a willingness to support the school in many ways, from fund-raising to facilitating school-wide activities. Dual-language families can also introduce the school community to cultural enrichment avenues such as the arts, music, and world cuisines, leveraging their community connections to help build strong after-school programs, better cafeterias, fulfilling field trips and site visits, internships, and more. A strong and well-prepared education argument can sometimes be the best way to convince minds and touch hearts.

Dual-language programs can give a new school or an underutilized school with empty classrooms a new identity. Having more quality choices in a district can also help relieve overcrowding in established competitive schools by attracting more middle-class families to currently disadvantaged schools and exploring the potential advantage of socioeconomic integration that dual-language programs may trigger. Grassroots initiatives can quickly mobilize hundreds of families to participate in combatting a school's dwindling population, as well as providing the means to boost a school's budget. In many districts, each new seat filled is attached to a budgetary increase. Sometimes, school districts or the Department of Education will even provide grants for planning, curriculum development, and professional development for teachers and staff. Additional financial and logistical help can also come to the school from partners and organizations that have a vested interest in the languages offered or the populations served (i.e. embassies, consulates, businesses, and foundations).

When you are granted an interview with a school principal you must present the data and the project in a very professional way. Explain the benefits to the children and the community as central to your initiative. Provide documents that will detail the demographics of incoming families by year and school zone. Explain the modalities of securing a dual-language grant from the Department of Education or from outside partners. After having met with a responsive principal, invite other players to show their support, especially other parents, teachers, and community members. Then, reach out to foreign government officials, elected officials, and donors. By following these steps, you will have built a very strong case for your project. In doing so, you will also have gained the trust of a community of parents and educators. Together you can now build a successful dual-language program.

Phase 3: Building a Successful Dual-Language Program from Day One

Once the principal is on board, you and your group must focus your attention on several important things. Above all, you will have to secure the required number of families and make sure that they enroll their children in the program. Organizing tours of the school and giving presentations during school events in order to enroll more families is a good idea, if space is available. You should also continue to promote the program by organizing ongoing parent information meetings and encouraging parents to visit existing dual-language schools. You can also bring established programs to your community by inviting dual-language teachers to share their experiences with interested parent and educator groups. Do not forget, you can also share best practices from established dual-language programs that you learned of during your site visits and interactions with other schools.

Securing the materials such as age-appropriate books and activities that will be needed by teachers in the first few months after the program is launched is a fantastic way to help your school principal and administration. You can support teachers by researching books that are aligned with the curriculum and preparing lists of items that can be ordered by the school or by other parents and supporters. If requested, you may need to assist the principal in the recruitment process, as finding competent and qualified bilingual teachers and teaching assistants often proves difficult. You may also be asked to help translate and interpret during interviews, as well as give your opinion on candidates' proficiency in the language. You are now an active member of the team, and your enthusiasm and willingness to help will play a significant role in the program's implementation and success.

If you have established a fundraising committee, they can start organizing events and drafting appeals to receive donations that will support the dual-language classroom, the library, and the school at large. In addition to providing resources, these funds can also be used to enlist the help of a dual-language specialist or consultant who will be able to train teachers and teacher assistants, develop the curriculum, and obtain instructional materials from vendors nationally or internationally. Finally, this group can also help with writing grant proposals in order to obtain additional funding from district, state, and federal agencies, foundations, and foreign governments.

Having a well-articulated and clear vision with which parents can identify helps to transcend cultural misunderstandings and invites families and communities to embrace your goals. When working with a school leader, it is important to be clear about the vision that the principal and the school board can craft. Ultimately, the principal is the one who is held accountable by all parties involved. Even if certain groups or individuals are not prepared to get on board immediately, this overarching vision can plant the seeds for further follow-up, whether it is related to fundraising, relationship building, or community partnerships. Many of the parents interviewed in the previous chapters saw their initiative as a young start-up that demanded time and constant nurturing.

The grassroots approach suggested above has been conceived through trial and error by parents and educators. It has served dozens of initiatives in various cities and in several linguistic communities, some of which are presented in the previous chapters. It has the potential to serve many more as it is finally available in a published form. This roadmap is an ever-evolving collection of lessons learned that continues to be improved upon and that, by nature, varies from school to school and from community to community—requiring users to make the necessary adjustments to fit their specific context. It was created by parents for parents. It exists because of the founding parents' strongly-held conviction that if it worked for them, it should be passed on to other parents so that more children can be afforded the gift of bilingual education. If this roadmap plays a role in your own initiative, do pass on your own version to others. In turn, they too can become the creators of successful programs that will benefit their children and improve their schools. The roadmap can fuel the Bilingual Revolution.

Chapter 12

Why Dual-Language Education
Is Good for Your Child

This chapter will serve as a primer for parents who are considering taking their first steps into the world of dual-language education. It will be equally useful to both monolingual parents and parents who already speak a language other than English, through their heritage or through their education, and wish to pass that gift on to their children. The information presented can be used later to develop a rationale to convince teachers, school administrators, and other parents and community members of the necessity for bilingual education in every school. Furthermore, this chapter will provide an overview of the unique characteristics of the bilingual brain and person, and will explain how being bilingual can help improve a child's ability to learn, focus, communicate, and understand the world.

Many of the advantages of bilingualism are intuitive. For instance, bilinguals can communicate with far more people around the globe and, as a result, have access to far more literary, academic, and artistic works, as well as professional and social networks, than monolinguals. Bilinguals also learn other languages more easily than their monolingual peers because after mastering a second language, individuals are able to call upon the strategies they employed to acquire a third or fourth language. Finally, bilingualism fosters an attitude of multiculturalism and open-mindedness. As world-renowned psycholinguist François Grosjean explains so eloquently, the identity of the bilingual "transcends national boundaries.[102]

What Does It Mean To Be Bilingual?

In the 1950s, linguists Uriel Weinreich and William Francis Mackey proposed that bilingualism is simply the "regular" use of two or more languages. In contrast, François Grosjean suggests that the ability to speak

99

more than one language is not just a linguistic skill. According to him, bilingualism constitutes a new and distinct identity. Both of these definitions highlight varying aspects of the bilingual person and the bilingual brain. Dual-language programs enable students to use more than one language in everyday life and in many different subject areas. They also empower heritage language speakers, as well as monolinguals, to either sustain their cultural and linguistic heritage or to develop new identities and skills of their own, thereby becoming a great source of pride within each community.

The term "heritage language" has been in use for about fifteen years. Its origins can be traced back to Quebec, Canada, later adopted into American educators' lexicons as they began to realize entire populations of students were unable to take advantage of language skills they had already acquired in their mother tongue. Instead of enrolling children in English as a Second Language (ESL) classes, which would often result in the erasure of a child's native language proficiency, educators realized that they could build on the language skills these children already brought to the classroom. Consequently, heritage language programs were born to develop literacy skills in both languages. This aim—to develop academic language proficiency in both English and the target language—is one of the major goals of the Bilingual Revolution.

At a recent public talk on bilingualism, language acquisition, and identity in New York, François Grosjean asserted: "The bilingual is a human communicator, a speaker, and a hearer in his or her own right who manages life with two or more languages."[103] In considering this definition, one might wonder whether this seemingly daunting task of "managing life" in more than one language is worth the struggle bilinguals inherently face. In other words, is bilingualism an asset or a liability, both for the student in the classroom and, later, for everyday life? What differences might there be between bilinguals and monolinguals, both in terms of their cognitive functions and their ways of navigating society? Just how important is it to be bilingual?

Bilingual people possess at least three spaces where they can "belong." These can be seen as aspects of tri-nationalism. In my own case, I feel French when using French, American when using English, and French-American when interacting with other bilinguals, and therefore using a mix of the two languages. Bilingualism opens doors to a wide range of cultures and communities that would have remained otherwise closed off to a monolingual person. Instead of having one linguistic "home" or comfort zone, bilinguals have many. As one might expect, a multilingual life is extraordinarily rich, diverse, and full of possibilities. As geographical barriers continue to dissolve in this era of globalization, borders no longer restrain the spread of ideas and cultures throughout the world. The complex identity of the bilingual is more relevant today than it has ever been, and will continue to play an increasingly important role in the future.

Keeping Bilingual Children Motivated

The motivation and desire to speak another language can be influenced by many different factors. Some come from the family environment. There are indeed families that achieve bilingualism painlessly thanks to a stimulating child-centered language experience at home. However, that is not always the case. For example, it is very common for bilingual parents to put too much pressure on their children to learn their own native language, sometimes even forcing a language to be spoken in family interactions. This desire might not be shared by the child. As a result, this approach often does not yield successful outcomes, for the parent or for the child. For home immersion to work, children should be surrounded with positive reinforcement so that they derive pleasure from learning the language and improving upon their skills.

Another important factor is community influence and the question of language status. If a child perceives the language spoken at home as having a lower status than the dominant language in their community, he or she may not want to be associated with it and may abstain completely from communicating or interacting in that language.[104] There are also individual personality factors linked to children's motivation and engagement in language experiences. Some children, at one point or another, do not want to speak their parents' language anymore. This can accompany youth and adolescent periods of rebellion, or develop as a result of peer pressure and wanting to fit in, among other reasons. In these situations, it is best to try to find an alternative way to motivate the child, one which takes into consideration his or her personal identity. It is imperative to take a child-centered approach by listening, engaging, and expanding on the reasons each child gives for wanting or not wanting to continue a specific language. In this way, the child can take ownership of their own learning and re-develop an interest in the language on their own terms.

The Bilingual Personality

In addition to the many cognitive advantages of knowing multiple languages, bilinguals often benefit from an increased emotional intelligence. Researchers such as psychologist and author Daniel Goleman describe this phenomenon as an increased self-awareness and awareness of others; a special capacity of bilinguals to better understand the perspective of another person through the cultural window of language; and an ability to experience a kind of empathy that is linguistically rooted but ultimately culturally experienced.[105] Emotions are an intrinsic and unique component of each language, highlighting why bilinguals are more adept at navigating and discerning a range of feelings across cultures. In the same vein, the ability to look at the same event or idea from a different linguistic and cultural perspective is enormously helpful in developing interpersonal relationships and navigating interactions with people of different backgrounds, both from within the same society and from around the world. Bilingualism is an investment with an incredible payoff. Speakers of two or more languages can readily be called upon when asked to brainstorm a new approach, try out a new idea, or understand a position that is different from their own. These tools help bilinguals navigate the complex globalized world with ease and operate on a more sophisticated level of understanding.

To these advantages, we should add a sense of accrued creativity observed in bilingual children, or to put it in more scientific terms, "divergent thinking." Author and international education expert Sir Kenneth Robinson's work on creativity offers valuable insights into divergent thinking by, for example, asking subjects how many uses they can think of for a paper clip.[106] In this exercise, divergent thinking is measured in three ways: (1) flexibility, or how many answers participants come up with, (2) originality, or how many original answers they provide, and (3) the level of detail provided, or how far participants can take each of their ideas. Many studies have compared how many answers monolinguals are able to give compared to bilinguals or multilinguals. The consensus is clear: bilingual and multilingual people excel at creative thinking and problem solving; they are consistently able to come up with more original uses for the paper clip scenario.[107] This is easily explained, as bilingualism is an expression of meaning-making—the process by which we interpret life events, make sense of relationships, and come to know ourselves. As bilinguals are skilled in juggling multiple expressions of similar feelings, objects, or experiences, it is convenient for them to utilize those skills to "think outside the box." Much to their advantage, bilinguals do not have just one box—they have multiple.

The Bilingual Edge

There are countless practical benefits to being bilingual. In recent years, important studies have examined how bilingual programs improve educational outcomes by analyzing how bilingual students learn. Researchers stress that bilingual students have a greater metalinguistic awareness[108]—in other words, they are more aware of language as a system—and process data with ease at the cognitive level. Because of these cognitive advantages, bilingual students demonstrate an increased control of attention, a longer memory span, and an aptitude to solve problems of above-average difficulty.[109]

Research also indicates that high school students in dual-language programs have lower dropout rates than those following monolingual curriculums.[110] Thomas and Collier conducted a longitudinal study over eighteen years in twenty-three school districts across fifteen states, comparing students in dual-language programs with students in transitional bilingual programs or English-only classes. They found that the dual-language model closed the achievement gap between English learners and native English speakers in both primary and secondary schools. The programs also transformed the school experience by promoting an inclusive community that appreciated and welcomed diversity.

These researchers concluded that dual-language learning is the only method of second language acquisition that facilitates the full closure of the achievement gap between English learners and English speakers in primary and secondary schools. Furthermore, bilingual students outperformed their monolingual peers on standardized tests—concrete evidence of the success of dual-language programs.[111] For these researchers, well-structured and well-implemented dual-language instruction across all subjects of the curriculum afforded all students the opportunity to develop a deep academic proficiency in both languages.[112]

Moreover, being bilingual at a young age can lead to many more opportunities to study and work abroad. Companies that employ bilingual people benefit materially with translation and interpretation services, facilitating communication with a larger clientele. In addition to the obvious assets of cultural and linguistic competencies, bilingual candidates are often preferred in the workforce as they have the ability to quickly adapt to new environments. These cutting-edge advantages can lead, subsequently, to higher salaries and more comprehensive access to the global job market.

In her pioneering work, Ellen Bialystok, research professor and chair in Lifespan Cognitive Development at York University, proved that bilingualism as an experience has a profound and clear impact on the structure and organization of the brain. She found that bilinguals benefit from lifelong advantages in problem solving thanks to the constant rewiring of their executive control system—a network of processes in the brain that gather information and structure it for evaluation, and take stock of our surroundings in order to adjust our behavior in response. Bilinguals' constant need to process information in two languages activates the executive control system more intensely. Their efforts to resolve problems or confusions for both verbal and nonverbal tasks in two language systems then reorganize that network. In the end, this reorganized network is more efficient than the monolingual equivalent. Bialystok also demonstrated that bilingualism is an outstanding source of cognitive reserve, an idea that refers to the way the brain is able to improve its performance through the use of cerebral connections. These studies highlight the very powerful ability of our daily experiences to fundamentally reshape the bilingual mind.

Research in neuroscience also highlights that learning to speak two languages from childhood is not only beneficial in regard to cognitive development and social opportunities, but also pays off in old age. Recent work by a team led by Ana Ines Ansaldo, director of the Brain Plasticity, Communication and Ageing Laboratory and professor at the University of Montreal, shows that, contrary to elderly monolinguals, elderly bilinguals performed problem-solving tasks with high success, without utilizing certain areas of the brain that are particularly vulnerable to aging. In a sense, lifelong bilingualism rewires the brain in such a way that it could be considered an insurance policy against age-related brain decline. [113]

The Family and Bilingualism

To achieve this level of bilingualism, the support of families is crucial because language is rooted in traditions and culture. Building an affinity for the culture behind the language is something that requires a lot of motivation for new language learners. The more the language can be rooted in the cultural experience—for example, through exposure to native speakers or the linkage between traditions and vocabulary words—the stronger the mastery of the language is. Many children in dual-language programs also attend weekend cultural enrichment programs, as their families seek out additional opportunities with emphasis on their home country's literature, culture, and history to foster a sense of belonging and pride as a member of that heritage group.

Parents are often concerned that children will become confused by speaking two languages beginning at a young age, and that this will negatively affect their ability to learn as they grow older. In reality, what people typically take as evidence of confusion is the fact that children, especially young ones, will very often mix the two languages in their speech, something that experts call "code-switching." For example, a child raised speaking Mandarin and English may start a sentence in Mandarin, throw in a word or two in English, and then continue on in Mandarin. The question is, does this really count as confusion? In an attempt to answer that question, about twenty years ago a group of linguists in Montreal studied instances where children seemed to be using the wrong language, or code-switching.[114] These experts found that not only are children who switch between languages not confused, but that code-switching is actually a very clever strategy that bilingual children employ. These young learners are simply utilizing all the linguistic resources they have at their disposal. In addition, it is important to remember that even monolingual children mix up words and meanings in their native language as they move through the various stages of language development. Knowing this now, code-switching no longer represents a cause for concern as it did before. The practice of code-switching can even be used to bilinguals' advantage, as it becomes second nature for them to adapt their language use to their surrounding environment.

In the language acquisition process, it is natural for children to model their speech off the individuals they hear speak most often—notably their parents. This can pose a problem if parents decide to speak to their children in a language they are not necessarily fluent or comfortable in. In the United States, some non-native English speaking parents choose to speak in English to their children because they suffered hardships or faced discrimination because of their accent or heritage. These parents want to ensure that their children speak English fluently, without an accent, to shield them from the adversity they themselves encountered. At the end of the day, it is more constructive for parents to speak to their children in their native language instead of in broken or grammatically-incorrect English. Each child's linguistic base must have a strong foundation—whether it is in English or in another language—that is derived from parental and familial communication at a very young age. This way, when the child enters school, teachers can build upon that language base to develop literacy in a second, or third, or fourth language. [115]

The Child and Bilingualism

When we, as adults, encounter two languages, whether in writing or in speech, we classify them as such—i.e. English and Spanish, or French and German. However, from the bilingual child's point of view, both languages comprise their total linguistic repertoire. Eventually, they are taught and learn how to select words from one specific language to accommodate the communicative terrain in which they are located. Sociolinguist Ofelia Garcia refers to this astute use of languages as "translanguaging." In bilingual classrooms, children develop one personal language system with different features that happen to have been socially assigned to two different languages. Garcia underscores that it is extremely important not to restrict language use to any one language. If we impede children from bringing their native language and their home experiences into the classroom, they are going to invent their own pidgin language (a mixture of simplified languages) or find some other way to communicate when they are together in groups. [116]

Often, teachers create separate language spaces—mainly for themselves, not for the children—to better organize their own teaching methods. Stories of imaginary lines that divide dual-language classrooms are common. If we are too strict with language separation, it does not benefit the child at all and actually limits their natural linguistic progression. Therefore, it is paramount to take care in developing successful bilingual programs and curricula.

One of the defining characteristics of dual-language programs is teaching Kindergarteners and 1st graders to read in their home language, whether it is English or the target language. Indeed, the fact that children can read in more than one language opens up worlds of learning opportunities, free from the limitations imposed by translations and inauthentic texts. In 2006, Stanford University professor Claude Goldenberg conducted five experimental studies and confirmed that learning in one's home language promotes reading achievement in a second language.

Because bilingual children use their languages in different situations, domains, and contexts, they may well have small vocabularies—especially when considering the languages independently. If all the family, home, and play vocabulary is in one language and all the school and academic vocabulary is in another, it is no surprise that children can develop a limited lexicon in each language. However, research indicates that when you consider the ensemble of both vocabularies, bilingual children are actually at a rather high level. Francois Grosjean calls this phenomenon the "complementarity principle," or the idea that bilinguals use different languages in different situations, with different people, in different contexts, to do different things. Of course, there can be overlap in languages in one or more domains—such as common interactions like greetings, small talk, and shopping. Other spheres of life are often covered by just one language—such as legal and business terms, academic jargon, or geographically-specific words. These linguistic realms grow with time as children develop more comprehensive vocabularies and learn to operate bilingually in more varied situations and contexts.

Nothing Is Perfect

While this chapter has focused mainly on the advantages of bilingualism, it would be amiss not to mention some of the possible drawbacks to living as a bilingual person. Many bilinguals, for example, report difficulties when communicating in their weaker language—especially in situations where they are not accustomed to using that language. Others have a hard time translating and suffer from a lack of vocabulary in one particular language. There are also cases where it can be difficult for bilinguals to be accepted for who they are—that is to say, members of two or more cultures speaking two or more languages—in each individual society they interact with. Nevertheless, the vast majority of bilinguals report their ability to speak more than one language to be an overwhelmingly positive experience. As such, it is fair to say that the advantages of bilingualism far outweigh these minor challenges.

The Potential of Bilingualism

When one considers the richness of this country's linguistic heritage and the number of linguistic communities that could benefit from dual-language programs, it is impossible not to see the gigantic potential for social change and collective advancement in the United States through the implementation of dual-language programs. Simply put, there are not enough dual-language programs offered, particularly when one acknowledges the advantages of dual-language education and the growing interest in bilingualism across the nation. The benefits of bilingualism can and should be extended to many more children so that they may lead prosperous, fulfilling, and enriched lives.

Chapter 13

Bilingual Education in the U.S.: Know Before You Go

The conversation surrounding bilingual education in the United States has often centered around the question of immigration. Historically, bilingual programs in the United States have largely been viewed as a means to aid immigrants' English language acquisition through a transitional model. Proponents of these programs do not focus on the advantages of mastering two languages, per se. In fact, these particular kinds of bilingual programs rarely place value on sustaining a heritage language, effectively failing to see the many advantages that learning in one's mother-tongue, as well as English, yields in an academic environment. Thankfully, despite this somewhat-established view of American bilingual education, attitudes and practices are beginning to change.

Dual-Language Programs for All and All for Dual-Language Programs

English as a Second Language (ESL) programs in the United States have traditionally, and understandably, focused on children whose household language is not English. However, as the ESL dominant model of English acquisition has begun to shift to a dual-language model, the objectives of these programs are evolving. Now, there are a growing number of dual-language programs created not only to serve English Language Learners, but also students for whom English is a native language. This can be explained by the overwhelming evidence that educating children in multiple languages offers a competitive advantage in the global economy, boosting not only their foreign language skills but also improving their English reading and comprehension, and even their math skills. These programs concentrate on the advantages of bilingualism for all students involved,

109

regardless of the language skills they come in with.

Dual-language programs in the United States are available in a wide range of languages. While English is always one of the two languages taught, programs can be found with target languages from Spanish, Mandarin, Korean, French, Japanese, German, Russian, Portuguese, Arabic, and Italian to Cantonese, Hmong, Bengali, Urdu, Creole, Cup'ik, and Ojibwe, to name but a few. Dual-language programs even exist in American Sign Language.[117] Each of the languages offered reflects the fiber of that particular community, which may include ethnic concentrations, commercial interests, or simply a desire to provide children a competitive advantage. In creating these programs, each community can make the United States, as a whole, more competitive academically and economically.

Bilingual education in the United States is multifaceted. With no federal law legislating the content of education, each school district controls decisions relating to its own pedagogy, while standards that affect curriculum development are defined at the state level. The resulting number and wide variety of bilingual programs can perplex parents and educators who wish to introduce similar programs to their communities. When discussing these programs, it is necessary to provide clear definitions for commonly employed terminology. Below are the definitions provided by the U.S. Department of Education's Office of English Language Acquisition:

- Two-way dual-language programs (also known as two-way immersion programs): English Language Learners who are fluent in the partner language and English-speaking peers are integrated to receive instruction in both English and the partner language.

- One-way dual-language programs: Students from predominantly one language group receive instruction in both English and a partner language. One-way dual-language programs may serve predominantly English Language Learners (also known as developmental or maintenance bilingual programs); predominantly English-speaking students (also known as one-way/world language immersion programs); or predominantly students with a family background or cultural connection to the partner language (also known as heritage or native language programs).[118]

There are also many subtle variations that shape each bilingual program, such as subjects taught and the duration of the program. With such a wide range of programs and languages, you are sure to find a model that works for your community and serves your local population in the best way possible.

Immigration and the Rise of Dual-Language Education: A Historical Perspective

The history of bilingual education in the United States rose and fell with the various waves of people that arrived at different points in time. From the early European arrivals at the turn of the seventeenth century, to the Puerto Ricans in the 1940s, to the massive exodus of Cubans in the early 1960s, American immigrant families' primary objective has not historically been to sustain their home languages but to gain access to English so that they could economically support themselves. At the time of these waves of immigration, home-language or heritage schools developed outside of, and in addition to, the public school system. Weekend and afternoon programs became methods of sustaining a certain level of linguistic and cultural heritage. However, the primary focus of in-school programs remained the mastery of English. Immigrant parents used these programs to navigate their new environment and ensure their and their children's success.

The immigration context, in turn, prompted legislation and judicial decisions that would have a significant impact on bilingual education. In 1965, immigration laws in the United States witnessed major reforms due to sweeping changes in demographics. The number of Chinese and East Asian immigrants increased rapidly—a population that did not speak English upon arrival in the United States. The growing Spanish-speaking population in America also realized the need for bilingual programs to serve their students. Unable to obtain access to the services necessary for their children to succeed in school, these immigrant communities began to realize that legal action was necessary to generate change in the public education system.

In New York City, Puerto Rican parents mobilized around ASPIRA (an advocacy organization that seeks to empower the Puerto Rican and Latino Community) and United Bronx Parents to fight for the rights of English Language Learners. Central to their movement was the notion that children's linguistic and cultural backgrounds comprised an essential component of effective pedagogy, and that both bilingual and cultural education should be implemented in public schools. In 1972, ASPIRA filed a civil rights lawsuit demanding that New York City provide classroom instruction in transitional Spanish for struggling Latino students. As a result, ASPIRA signed a consent decree with the NYC Board of Education in 1974, considered a landmark lawsuit in the history of bilingual education in the United States, which established bilingual instruction as a legally-enforceable federal entitlement for New York City's non-English-speaking Puerto Rican and Latino students.[119]

Also in 1974, a group of Chinese-American students in San Francisco brought forth a civil rights case based on the claim that they were denied equal opportunity in education, which they argued they were entitled to under Title VI of the Civil Rights Act of 1964 that forbids discrimination on the basis of national origin. Ruling in favor of the students in what is now known as the *Lau v. Nichols* case, the Supreme Court affirmed that these students should receive equity in public school education. This landmark case has become a legal basis for English Language Learner students and their families to demand bilingual programs in their native language in the United States, as is detailed in some of the vignettes presented earlier in this book. *Lau v. Nichols* reflects, among other things, the now widely-accepted view that a person's language is closely intertwined with his or her national origin, and that language-based discrimination is effectively a proxy for origin-based discrimination.[120]

A few years after *Lau v. Nichols* and the end of the Vietnam War, a new wave of refugee immigration swept through the United States as a result of the Southeast Asian Immigration Act of 1979. In particular, the Gulf of Mexico coast became home to thousands of Vietnamese speakers, while Hmong speakers from Northern Vietnam, Laos, and Cambodia resettled in Minnesota.[121] Today, as a result of this massive migration, Minnesota has the United States' largest Hmong-speaking population and the largest number of Hmong bilingual programs.[122] Refugees resettled from different war zones have also helped revitalize several American communities, notably Bosnians in Utica, New York; Somalis in Lewiston, Maine; and Syrians in Detroit, Michigan.

Overcoming the Bilingual Taboo in America

At its core, America's monolingual problem lies in where the United States is physically situated. Unlike most of the rest of the world, where it is typical for populations to share borders with numerous linguistic communities, opportunities for language exchange in the United States are limited by its geographical vastness. The United States is consequently more apt to be self-contained. In addition, the United States is a very wealthy and well-positioned country, in terms of economic opportunities and standard of living, and as such many Americans feel no need to learn a second language to improve their personal or professional situation.

Despite Americans' monolingual mentality, experts agree that the foreign language deficit in the United States impedes its global competitiveness.[123] Foreign language programs are unfortunately seldom introduced before high school, despite the fact that it is far easier for young children in elementary school to quickly learn new languages. The epitome of the American language crisis came after 9/11 when it was revealed that telling messages in Arabic intercepted by U.S. intelligence were not interpreted on time due to a lack of translators. The U.S. Department of State subsequently began to fund "critical language" summer immersion programs in languages such as Arabic, Chinese, Russian, Japanese, and Korean.[124] However, in targeting college students far beyond the prime age for fluent language acquisition, this effort has not had the impact that it could have. Shorter language immersion programs, such as summer camps, have also increased in popularity but tend to produce varying results.

In the 1990s and early 2000s, bilingual programs came under attack for their supposed lack of effectiveness in teaching English to immigrants, and ballot campaigns succeeded in banning transitional bilingual education programs in California, Massachusetts, and Arizona.[125] This resulted in the increased stigmatization of Latinos, Asians, Pacific Islanders, Africans, West Indians, Native Americans, and other language minority groups. It also gave strength to the English-only movement, which unfortunately continues to this day to actively influence many members of Congress in their efforts to push through monolingual policies.[126] Despite this adversity, schools were able to find loopholes and begun adopting "dual-language" models—cleverly disguising the charged term "bilingual," which had taken on a politicized negative meaning.

Dual-language programs are now beginning to thrive. Georgia, Delaware, and North Carolina, among other states, have expanded their investments in dual-language immersion; Minnesota has revised its budget and educational policies to benefit young dual-language learners; New York and Oregon are changing their strategic approaches to long-term academic outcomes for bilingual children; legislators in California and Massachusetts have proposed overturning their respective bans on bilingual education, and the list goes on. The fact that bilingual education is once again becoming a political issue, this time with overwhelming support, is an indicator of the success of these programs.

In 2000, then-Secretary of Education Richard Riley called for the number of dual-language programs in the United States to grow from an estimated 260 in 2000 to a projected 1,000 by 2005—which, according to the Center for Applied Linguistics' databases on two-way and one-way immersion programs, clearly has been reached.[127] Current unverified estimates even approach 2,000 dual-language programs in the United States.[128] This growth points to the success of dual-language education, in spite of the "bilingual taboo."

A State-led Path to a Bilingual Future

Uniquely, Utah boasts the third highest number of dual-language programs in the United States with approximately 140 schools serving 34,000 students, as of 2017. An anomaly of sorts, bilingual programs in Utah—a state geographically isolated from important economic centers—have thrived despite a lack of diverse linguistic communities. Foreign language immersion in Utah was conceived, championed, and implemented thanks to the vision of strong political figures who identified a need for language skills in business, government, and education. In 2008, the Utah Senate passed the International Education Initiative, providing funding for Utah schools to begin dual-language immersion programs in Chinese, French, and Spanish. German, and Portuguese were later added to the curricular offerings, and Arabic and Russian are in the planning stages for the near future.[129]

The Utah dual-language immersion initiative uses a partial immersion model, where students receive fifty percent of their instruction in the target language and the other fifty percent in English, with two teachers per each class. Most of Utah's programs begin in 1st grade, with a select few starting in Kindergarten. By high school, participating students are expected to enroll in Advanced Placement language coursework and pass the AP World Languages and Cultures exams in the 9th grade. In grades 9 through 12, students will eventually be offered university-level coursework through blended learning opportunities with six major universities in Utah. The study of a third language in high school is also encouraged. This full continuum of programs is an important step in the evolutionary process of bilingual education.

The Negative Impact of Ending Too Early

Across the country, bilingual programs in public schools tend to stop at the upper elementary school level, and very few continue on to middle school. Even if the programs continue past the elementary level, the majority tend to offer more hours in the target language when the children are younger, and then add more hours in English as they progress to middle school or high school. This is truly a shame because, even if dual-language programs provide excellent opportunities for language learning at the elementary school level, this lack of an educational continuum greatly diminishes the value of the skills the children gain at a young age, as they risk a grave loss of knowledge. Of note, I have been actively engaged with the Boerum Hill School for International Studies—a public middle and high school in Brooklyn—in seeking to remedy this problem by combining an International Baccalaureate program with dual-language program in French and English from grades 6 to 12. Our goal is that the students will be able to graduate with a bilingual IB diploma in order to prepare them for college careers at top universities around the world. Collaborative efforts such as these are the key to maintaining the bilingualism young children achieve, and caring for the precious gift of language.

As globalization pushes our world closer together than ever before, we must reflect on our competitiveness at an international level. Knowledge of multiple languages and cultures can give Americans that edge, as cohorts upon cohorts of high school and college graduates are capable of entering the workforce better equipped for the global market. Bilingual education has been proven time and time again to produce incredible results, but the field is stalled in the United States by a lack of mobilization on the national level fueled by disproved myths and taboos. The Bilingual Revolution is needed now more than ever to establish the prominent position of bilingual education, for posterity's sake.

The Future of Education
is in Two Languages

Over the past fifteen years, linguistic communities in various cities across the United States have created and supported scores of dual-language programs that provide instruction in dozens of languages, some of which have been highlighted in the previous chapters. The stories in this book illustrate the passion and enthusiasm shared by all those involved in the implementation of these programs, and prove that it is indeed possible to create a dual-language program from the ground up. By sharing the stories of the New York Bilingual Revolution and the roadmap that parents and educators used along the way, it is my hope this book can become a source of guidance for parents and educators who are considering similar programs for their schools. The stories of the Japanese, Italian, German, Russian, Arabic, Polish, Spanish, Chinese, and French dual-language initiatives in New York City unfolded in different ways, yet all yield similar advice: the vision of a small few has the power to galvanize an entire movement to bring bilingual education to new communities in public schools across the nation and around the globe. These programs are more than just language programs. They build cultural awareness in schools by generating cross-cultural exchanges. They strengthen and support heritage languages in our communities. They promote the values of linguistic and cultural diversity for every society in the 21st century and beyond.

When we think about the "global world" in which we live today, we can no longer cling to the notion that only speaking English is good enough. Simply put, the United States is falling behind and missing out. People all over the world are learning English and becoming multilingual themselves. It is imperative that we in the United States be able to read, write, and communicate in more than one language. If we cannot move forward from our current complacency, both we and our children will miss out on the wealth of personal, social, professional, and academic benefits bilingualism affords. As the former World Language and Dual-Language Immersion Specialist for the Utah State Office of Education, Gregg Roberts, once put it: "Monolingualism is the illiteracy of the 21st century."

Most non-English speakers who come to the United States lose their home language within two generations. Grandchildren and grandparents lose the ability to communicate with each other. It is even possible for children and parents to lose their ability to communicate with each other in meaningful ways. Many of the families presented in this book were not willing to stand idly by when faced with this crisis. These parents believed in the cross-generational benefits of preserving their heritage, thereby unlocking troves of literature, culture, and history, as well as fostering a sense of belonging, pride, and identity. These parents understood that dual-language programs could contribute to a vibrant, rich, and diverse society. Above all, they understood that bilingualism is about families. It is about sustaining who we are in powerful ways that transcend language learning itself.

In our present society, English holds the power to wipe out other languages—languages that are incredibly valuable and that carry rich cultures, and histories, and knowledge. Along with this linguistic dominance come the forces of Americanization and assimilation, both of which are often carried to extremes. Although language learning is a global concern, the Bilingual Revolution begins locally in neighborhoods, schools, and communities. Without having to be told, many children figure out the enormous weight that English carries in our monolingual environment. The result is often that their native language appears in a new and negative light. Instead of succumbing to this pressure, we have to teach them, their parents, their schools, and their communities that being bilingual is best. The more we can communicate within our own communities, as well as with others, the stronger the fabric of our society will be.

As we have seen in this book, it is not always easy to create dual-language programs from the bottom up. That being said, if parents follow the roadmap and school authorities develop clearer guidelines and support mechanisms, grassroots initiatives of this kind will be able to operate more effectively and become more likely to succeed. The hardships, endurance, and perseverance portrayed in these dual-language initiatives are indicators that our entire educational system in the United States today must be transformed into something quite different from what it is now. Schools must meet the growing demand for dual-language education by embracing it wholeheartedly.

In the cases examined in this book, it was parents who worked tirelessly to successfully integrate dual-language programs into their schools. It was parents who devoted tremendous amounts of time, effort, and commitment to their endeavors. It was parents who researched, planned, and implemented these new programs at their local schools. It was parents who formed well-oiled machines and designed remarkable strategies to locate and target schools, and recruit families. Even when the groundwork was laid and their dual-language program did not crystallize in a timely manner, parents forged on. Despite the hurdles, set-backs, and seemingly endless bureaucratic red tape, these parents, along with school administrators and teachers, did not give up. This group has taken their communities, and even their country, quantum leaps forward.

As with any revolution, there are several significant challenges to overcome in order to reproduce it on a large scale. At the heart of these challenges are schools' funding and budgets. Almost all the schools approached by parents in this book discussed their need for additional financial resources to accommodate such programs. Access to educational materials in the target language is another recurring problem faced by dual-language educators. The scarcity and cost of essential educational materials present serious hurdles for schools, especially for those that lack adequate resources. To overcome these challenges, collaboration between school administrators, foundations, and local community organizations that can provide funding is of paramount importance. Much of the success of dual-language education lies in the unwavering support of these fruitful partnerships.

An equally-significant challenge emanates from the difficulty of recruiting and engaging bilingual teachers. Laws regarding the necessary requirements to teach in public schools in the United States vary from state to state. This narrows the field of candidates significantly. National certifications, instead of state-held ones, would significantly help to combat this administrative hurdle. Further complicating the matter, a limited pool of bilingual teachers are U.S. citizens or green card holders. While schools can offer various visas to teachers they are in the process of recruiting, they are only temporary. Some states only allow the use of this mechanism if no other American state-certified teacher is qualified to do the same job. This significantly reduces schools' options, especially if they wish to recruit native speakers of the target language in order to create a more immersive environment. This problem is exacerbated in schools far from major urban centers. Luckily, there is a long-term solution to this issue. As students currently in dual-language programs eventually graduate from college and become teachers themselves, they have the potential to become capable, qualified, and certified bilingual teachers. This potential future cohort of competent bilingual educators can change everything. Once bilingualism becomes the rule instead of the exception, qualified candidates become less hard to find. Once given time to grow, dual-language programs become sustainable programs.

There are some definite and heartening signs that Americans are beginning to broaden their horizons, to think beyond the confines of their own country, and to recognize the richness and diversity that is a part of their culture today. It is becoming increasingly common for Americans to speak a language other than English at home, thanks in part to immigration. Being fluent in more than one language is slowly becoming more of the norm, especially in urban centers. At the same time, bilingualism has experienced a surge in interest as parents learn of the advantages that early foreign language learning can offer their children. The cognitive, academic, social, personal, and professional advantages of bilingualism are undeniable. Bilingualism and multilingualism are now viewed as an asset, not just for their cultural virtues, but also for their ability to produce global citizens. There should be no question: a bilingual education should be available to every child, in the United States and around the world.

The Bilingual Revolution was built on a foundation laid by parents. Now, the power is in your hands. The roadmap and stories featured in this book are for you. Learn from their successes and from their failures. Use them to inspire and engage your community. Through it all, know you are backed by a global movement that believes in the power of bilingualism. With sincere optimism and hope, I proudly pass the torch of the Bilingual Revolution to you. The future of education may be in two languages, but it is our future to create.

Appendix

The Roadmap
(abridged)

This is an abridged roadmap for parents who are interested in creating a dual-language program in a public school. Parents can make a difference in their communities, by starting dual-language programs no matter where they are located.

This roadmap is divided into three phases:

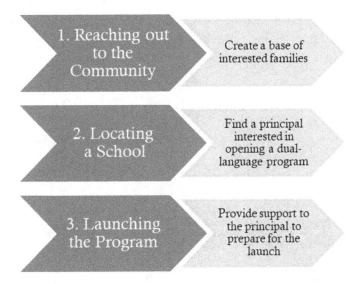

Phase One
Reaching Out to the Community:
Creating a Base of Interested Families

To make this work you'll need to connect with dozens, if not hundreds, of individuals in your community to form a base of interested families. You can start by forming a core group of parents you know and trust. These are parents who will take part in your shared vision even if they do not have children who will benefit from this initiative.

If you are not initiating this endeavor with a target language already in mind, but are interested in dual-language education as a way to educate your child, it is preferable to research your community's linguistic heritage in order to gauge the support you might receive. Understanding the cultural nuances upon which a specific community will judge your proposal will be key, and identifying partners and fellow educational entrepreneurs from within the target culture will help to facilitate your project by presenting it in a way that is typically acceptable or preferred by a community.

Ways to reach out and find interested families include:

- Make a public announcement through social media, community and parenting blogs, letters, flyers, posters, or word of mouth that you are looking for people who are interested in helping you to create a dual-language program in a specific language.
- Look for existing community networks of businesses, religious centers, community centers, and children who are native speakers of another language within the parameters of your school district.
- Distribute a letter or flyer when you attend meetings or give presentations.
- Contact local preschools and daycare centers, Head-Start programs, private schools, language schools, cultural centers, religious institutions, parent associations, and city agencies that support families.
- Engage in conversations with parents at local playgrounds, in stores, at supermarkets, and in schools where families might be looking for options for younger siblings.
- Wear clothes, hats, or badges that will pique other parents' curiosity.

Once your group has gathered enough volunteers, you can start organizing committees to divide up the various tasks. Several committees can be organized, including: a community outreach committee, a school location committee, and a curriculum support committee. Additional committees can also be included at various stages of the process based on the initiative's more urgent needs, i.e. a teacher recruitment committee, a fundraising committee, or an after-school program committee, to name a few.

Collecting Data

Your community outreach committee should focus on gathering family data on:

- The number of families potentially interested in the program,
- The languages spoken at home and understood by the children,
- Children's dates of birth and their anticipated entry into primary school
- Families' school district or school zone

This data collection will also help you determine whether the dual-language program that you will be supporting will be one-way or two-way:

- One way: with only one group of children speaking the same language and receiving instruction in another.
- Two-way: with two groups of children split into one group whose home language is the program's target language and another group whose language is the official or national language, in this case English.

This decision will be based on the number of native speakers that you will enroll. To set a target number of students you will need to verify the average number of children enrolled in an entering grade in your school district and the mandate under which a school district operates with regard to non-native speakers it has of the national or official language.

Thus, your research may need to:

- Determine the number of children by school district or zone considered non-native speakers or English learners.
- Determine the number of children by school district or zone considered bilingual.
- Determine the number of children by school district or zone considered native speakers of the national or official language (in this case, English) who have no knowledge of the target language but whose families are

committed to dual-language education in the target language that you have set.

This data will help you explain how your dual-language program will serve different needs. Doing so may also help you secure additional funding from state agencies or philanthropic organizations, particularly those that support English Language Learners.

Frequently, potential enrollment will start off with a large base and end up with a small group on opening day. It is advisable that you recruit more students than are necessary to open a bilingual program in your local schools.

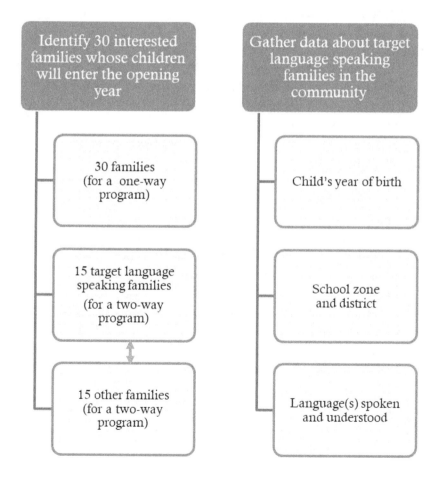

Community Outreach

A critically important task to undertake early in your effort is to create a support-base in the community, such as influential individuals, elected officials, supportive organizations.

This involves:

- Attending community meetings and informing the public about the dual-language program initiative.
- Booking an appointment with school officials (State Department of Education, District Superintendent, Office of Language Learners, etc.) to show your data and answer questions.
- Including school principals in these meetings as well to assess how they value dual-language education.
- Exchanging information with parent associations, parent coordinators, and teachers.
- Reaching out to community education councils, school boards, community boards, and local Council members.
- Organizing small gatherings at local coffee shops, restaurants, bakeries, at home, or in public spaces to pitch your ideas, gauge interest, or recruit potential families. In the case of such a gathering, you can invite one or all of the above-mentioned stakeholders to give a speech or share remarks.
- Connecting with embassies, consulates, honorary consuls, cultural centers serving a language or a country, foundations with a focus on education or community development, tourism offices, international or joined chambers of commerce that serve businesses from two or more countries, and heritage and cultural societies and federations.

Curriculum Support Committee

Your curriculum support committee can provide assistance at various stages during the process:

- Compiling and sharing information about the benefits of dual-language education during information sessions with parents in the community.
- Site visits to existing dual-language programs to determine best practices and to see first-hand how a program is administered.
- Interactions with already-established dual-language programs to ask questions about parental involvement and loyalty, sustainability, fundraising, and needs in terms of resources, teachers, and administrative support.
- Meeting and inviting parents who have succeeded in creating a dual-language program to learn from their experiences.

Phase 2
Developing a Convincing Rationale and Locating a Host School

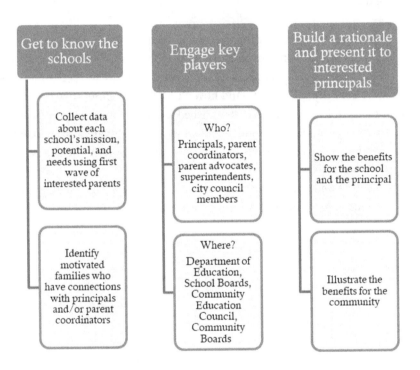

At the end of their collaborative work, the various committees must be prepared to present the data to a principal and then to the school community. Before approaching a school principal with your idea, it is advisable to build a local strategy and a persuasive argument that will help you convince the school principal as well as other appropriate administrators of the importance of your proposal.

Arguments in favor of dual-language programs include:

- A new principal might be seeking recognition and a dual-language program would be a concrete way to leave their mark on the school, and even the community.
- A successful program can bring a lot of positive visibility to a school, advance its reputation, and attract new sources of funding.
- Dual-language programs impart a lifelong gift of a second language to all children of the community.
- For second or third-generation families, dual-language programs safeguard their language and cultural heritage, and enable them to share these with all children.
- Highly motivated families join the school each year, and bring with them a willingness to support the school in many ways from fund-raising to facilitating school-wide activities.
- Dual-language families can also introduce the school community to cultural elements such as the arts, music and gastronomy—leveraging their community connections to help build strong after-school programs, better cafeterias, field trips and site visits, internships, and more.
- Dual-language can give a new school or an under-utilized school with empty classrooms a new identity.
- Having more quality choices in the district can also help relieve overcrowding in already-established competitive schools, by attracting more middle-class families to currently disadvantaged schools, and exploring the potential advantage of socioeconomic integration that dual-language programs may trigger.
- Sometimes, a school district or the Department of Education will provide grants for planning, curriculum development, and professional development for teachers and staff.
- Additional financial and logistical help can also come to the school from partners and organizations that have a vested interest in the languages offered or the populations served (i.e. embassies, consulates, businesses, and foundations).

When you are granted an interview with a school principal you must present the data and the project in a very professional way. Explain the benefits to the children and the community as being central to your initiative. Provide documents that will detail the demographics of incoming families by year and school zone. Explain the modalities of securing a dual-language grant from the Department of Education or from outside partners. After having met with a responsive principal, invite other players to come in and show their support, especially other parents, teachers, and community members. Then, reach out to foreign government officials, elected officials, and donors. By following these steps, you will have built a very strong case for your project, and you will have gained the trust of a community of parents and educators. Together you can now build a successful dual-language program.

Phase 3
Building a Successful Dual-Language Program
from Day One

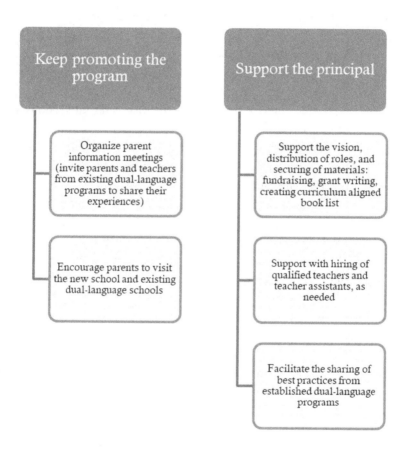

Once the school principal is on board, you and your group must focus your attention on several other aspects:

- Most importantly, you will have to secure the required number of families and make sure that they enroll their children in the program.
- Organize tours of the school and give presentations during school events in order to enroll more families, if space is

available.

- Continue to promote the program
- Organize ongoing parent information meetings
- Invite parents and teachers from existing dual-language programs to share their experiences.

There are also a number of ways you can support the principal:

- Secure the materials that will be needed by teachers in the first few months after the program is launched.
- Share best practices from established dual-language programs that you acquired during your site visits and interactions with other schools.
- Research books that are aligned with the curriculum, and prepare lists of books that can be ordered by the school or by other parents and supporters.
- You may need to assist the principal in the recruitment process, as finding competent and qualified bilingual teachers and teaching assistants is often difficult.
- You may be asked to help with translating and interpreting during interviews, as well as giving your opinion on the candidates' proficiency in the language.

The fundraising committee can start a number of tasks as well, such as:

- Organizing events and drafting appeals to receive donations that will support the dual-language classroom, the library, and the school at large.
- Enlisting the help of a dual-language specialist or a consultant who will be able to train teachers and teacher assistants, develop the curriculum, and obtain instructional materials from vendors nationally or internationally.
- Helping to write grant proposals in order to obtain additional funding from district, state, federal agencies, foundations, and foreign governments.

Resources

thebilingualrevolution.info

- Join the community, contribute, and support
- Access videos, testimonials, reading suggestions
- Sign up for The Bilingual Revolution newsletter
- Download resources such as ready-to-use or customizable presentations and brochures
- Locate existing programs
- Identify fellow revolutionaries near you, and form a new group
- Order posters and materials
- Sign up for webinars
- Gain access to experts
- Sponsor a translation of this book
- Buy books in bulk for fairs, events, conferences

Notes

Notes to Introduction

1 Elizabeth A. Harris, New York City Education Department to Add or Expand 40 Dual-Language Programs. New York Times, 14 January 2015.

2 For more information on mandates and bilingual education policies by state, visit the website of New America.

3 U.S. Department of Education, Dual-Language Education Programs: Current State Policies and Practices

Notes to Chapter 1

4 The following legal precedents have had a significant impact on bilingual education in the United States, and in granting children with limited English proficiency the right to receive instruction in their native tongue and in English: *Meyer v. Nebraska*; *Lau v. Nichols*; *Serna v. Portales*; *Aspira v. N.Y. Board of Education*; *Keyes v. School District No. 1, Denver, Colorado*; *Flores v. Arizona*; *Castaneda v. Pickard*. Read also The Bilingual Education Act and No Child Left Behind which have also impacted bilingual education.

5 For more information on this topic, read Christine Hélot & Jürgen Erfurt, *L'éducation bilingue en France : politiques linguistiques, modèles et pratiques*

6 Helen Ó Murchú, The Irish language in education in the Republic of Ireland.

7 Canadian Parents for French, The State of French-Second-Language Education in Canada 2012: Academically Challenged Students and FSL Programs

8 Interview with Robin Sundick. Principal of P.S.84. July, 10 2015.

9 To learn more on this topic, read Thomas & Collier, The Astounding Effectiveness of Dual-Language Education for All.

10 Interview with Heather Foster-Mann, Principal of PS 133, excerpted from a French Embassy report on French dual-language programs in the United States.

11 Interview with Marie Bouteillon, former Teacher at P.S.58 and Consultant in dual-language programming and curriculum design. May 19, 2016.

12 For instance, a 501(c) organization in the United States which is a tax-exempt nonprofit organization that can receive unlimited

contributions from individuals, corporations, and unions. The most common type of tax-exempt nonprofit organization falls under category 501(c)(3) in the U.S. Internal Revenue Code, whereby a nonprofit organization is exempt from federal income tax if its activities have the following purposes: charitable, religious, educational, scientific, literary, testing for public safety, fostering amateur sports competition, or preventing cruelty to children or animals.

13 Interview with Gretchen Baudenbacher, parent and PTA President at P.S.110. March 1, 2016.

Notes to Chapter 2

14 Interview with Yuli Fisher, January 26, 2016
15 Verdugo Woodlands Elementary and Dunsmore Elementary School in the Glendale Unified School District
16 Interview with Aya Taylor, Program Specialist at the Glendale Unified School District. January 22, 2016.
17 Interview with Jeffrey Miller, Director of Education and Family Programs at the Japan Society. January 19, 2016.
18 Interview with Yumi Miki, parent and co-founder of the JDLP initiative. January 19, 2016.
19 Interview with Hee Jin Kan, parent and co-founder of the JDLP. February 2, 2016.
20 Interview with Yuli Fisher, January 26, 2016
21 Interview with Yuli Fisher, January 26, 2016
22 Interview with Monica Muller, parent at P.S. 147 and co-founder of the JDLP. February 23, 2016.
23 501(c)3See discussion and definition in Chapter 3
24 Interview with Mika Yokobori, parent at P.S. 147. January 15, 2016.

Notes to Chapter 3

25 Interview with Marcello Lucchetta, January 25, 2016
26 Interview with Marcello Lucchetta, January 25, 2016
27 Interview with Jack Spatola, Principal of P.S. 172, March 9, 2016
28 Interview with Joseph Rizzi, Program Director at the Federation of Italian-American Organizations. November 13, 2016
29 Interview with Louise Alfano, Principal of P.S. 112. November 13, 2016
30 Excerpted from Rachel Silberstein, New York's First Italian Dual-Language Preschool Coming To Bensonhurst (Bensonhurst Bean).

Notes to Chapter 4

31 Interview with Gabi Hegan, Founder of CityKinder. February 19, 2016.
32 Interview with Sylvia Wellhöfer. January, 29 2016.
33 Ibid.

Notes to Chapter 5

34 Out of many, one (the motto of the United States).
35 American Community Survey 2015
36 Interview with Tatyana Kleyn, Professor of Bilingual Education at the City College of New York. March 11, 2016.
37 I.S. stands for intermediate school, which caters grades 6, 7 and 8.
38 Interview with Maria Kot, former parent at P.S. 200. March 4, 2016
39 Ibid.
40 Interview with Julia Stoyanovich and Olga Ilyashenko, February 25, 2016

Notes to Chapter 6

41 French Morning and France-Amérique
42 For more information on this story, see Jane Ross and Fabrice Jaumont, Building bilingual communities: New York's French bilingual revolution.
43 Amy Zimmer, How schools' French dual-language programs are changing NYC neighborhoods. DNA Info, May 26, 2015
44 Interview with Virgil de Voldère, parent at P.S.84. April 10, 2013.
45 Interview with Talcott Camp, parent at P.S.84. June 10, 2016.
46 Founded in 1904, the Société des Professeurs de Français et Francophones d'Amérique supports teachers and researchers interested in the French language and Francophone cultures
47 Founded in 1955, FACE is a non-profit 501(c)3 dedicated to nurturing French-American relations through innovative international projects in the arts, education, and cultural exchange. Housed in the Cultural Services of the French Embassy in New York, and overseen by a Board of Trustees, FACE serves an extensive network of patrons through its film-based programs and provides support to various initiatives through its partnership with the Cultural Services of the French Embassy.
48 Kirk Semple, A big advocate of French in New York's schools: France. NY Times, January 30, 2014.
49 Internationals Network for Public Schools is an educational nonprofit supporting International high schools and academies, serving newly arrived immigrants who are English language learners in New York,

California, Kentucky, Maryland, Virginia, and Washington, DC. Internationals Network also partners with other schools and districts across the country.

Notes to Chapter 7

50 Donna Nevel, The Slow Death of Khalil Gibran International Academy. (Chalkbeat)
51 Ibid.
52 Andrea Elliott, Muslim educator's dream branded a threat in the U.S. (NY Times)
53 Retrieved from the school's website on 8/26/2016
54 Randa Kayyali. The people perceived as a threat to security: Arab Americans since September 11.
55 Interview with Zeena Zakharia. June 23, 2016
56 Ibid.
57 Interview with Carine Allaf, Director of Programs at the Qatar Foundation International. February 2, 2016.
58 Interview with Mimi Met, Independent Consultant. March 8, 2016.
59 "Our Mission", retrieved from the organization's website on August 10, 2016.
60 Ibid.
61 Retrieved from the "I Speak Arabic" website on August, 5 2016.
62 Karen Zeigler and Steven Camarota, One in five U.S. Residents speaks foreign language at home.
63 Interview with Carol Heeraman, Principal of P.S./I.S. 30. March 8, 2016

Notes to Chapter 8

64 American Community Survey, 2015.
65 William Galush, For more than bread: Community and identity in American Polonia, 1880–1940.
66 Christopher Gongolski and Michael Cesarczyk, Two languages, one home. (Greenpoint News)
67 Interview with Julia Kotowski, parent at P.S.34. June 16, 2016
68 Interview with Elizabeth Czastkiewicz, Kindergarten teacher at P.S. 34. June 16, 2016.
69 Interview with Carmen Asselta, Principal of PS34. June 16, 2016.
70 Interview with Elizabeth Czastkiewicz, Kindergarten teacher at P.S. 34. June 16, 2016.
71 Interview with Alicja Winnicki, Superintendent of District 14. June 6, 2016
72 Interview with Julia Kotowski, parent at P.S. 34. June 16, 2016
73 Interview with Carmen Asselta, Principal of P.S. 34. June 16, 2016.

74 Interview with Alicja Winnicki, Superintendent of District 14. June 6, 2016
75 Ibid.

Notes to Chapter 9

76 Interview with Ofelia Garcia, Professor at the CUNY Graduate School. June 14, 2016.
77 Interview with Carmen Dinos, May 19, 2015
78 Ibid.
79 Milady Baez, NYC Deputy Schools Chancellor, keynote address to Russian Dual-Language Program gathering at Columbia University in New York. May 12, 2016.
80 Ibid.
81 NYC Department of Education, Chancellor Fariña names 15 schools Model Dual-Language Programs
82 Retrieved from the school's website on August 20, 2016.
83 Carla Zanoni, Principal Miriam Pedraja teaches uptown children two languages at a time. (Chalkbeat)
84 Interview with Maria Jaya, founding parent and co-director of Cypress Hills Community School. September 19, 2016.
85 For more information on the school, read Laura Ascenzi-Moreno and Nelson Flores, A Case Study of Bilingual Policy and Practices at the Cypress Hills Community School
86 U.S. News Report High School Rankings: High School for Dual Language and Asian Studies. Retrieved from U.S. News website on August 23, 2016.
87 "Mission" retrieved from the school's website on August 23, 2016.
88 Excerpted from Castellón, M., Cheuk, T., Greene, R., Mercado-Garcia, D., Santos, M., Skarin, R. & Zerkel, L. Schools to Learn from: How Six High Schools Graduate English Language Learners College and Career Ready.

Notes to Chapter 10

89 Interview with Ron Woo, Professor at Bank Street College, and Consultant at the NYU Metropolitan Center for Research on Equity and the Transformation of Schools. June 16, 2015.
90 The China Institute in America is a nonprofit educational and cultural institution in New York City that was founded in 1926 by a group of distinguished American and Chinese educators including John Dewey, Hu Shih, Paul Monroe and Dr. Kuo Ping-wen. It is the oldest bicultural organization in America devoted exclusively to China.
91 Founded in 1956 by John D. Rockefeller 3rd, Asia Society is the leading educational organization dedicated to promoting mutual

understanding and strengthening partnerships among peoples, leaders and institutions of Asia and the United States in a global context.

92 Interview with Li Yan, Principal of The High School for Dual Language and Asian Studies, September 14, 2016.

93 Interview with Ron Woo, Professor at Bank Street College, and Consultant at the NYU Metropolitan Center for Research on Equity and the Transformation of Schools. June 16, 2015.

94 Interview of Thalia Baeza Milan retrieved from Patrick Wall, City to add dozens of dual-language programs as they grow in popularity. (Chalkbeat)

95 Excerpted from Castellón, M., Cheuk, T., Greene, R., Mercado-Garcia, D., Santos, M., Skarin, R. & Zerkel, L., Schools to Learn from: How Six High Schools Graduate English Language Learners College and Career Ready.

96 For more information, updates, resources and examples on this topic, visit the official website of The Bilingual Revolution.

Notes to Chapter 11

97 Gratitude is expressed to the parents of the Downtown French DLP initiative, the parents and teachers of PS84 in Manhattan and PS58 in Brooklyn, the members of Education en Français à New York, the founders of La Petite Ecole, and the education office of the Embassy of France. Gratitude is also expressed to the parents of the Japanese, German, Italian, French and Russian DLP initiatives, presented in the next chapters, who have shared their version of the roadmap or helped improve the original version.

98 The numbers cited in this text reflect those in New York City where schools usually enroll a maximum of 18 children per class in pre-Kindergarten, about twenty-four children per class in Kindergarten, and over 30 children per class in secondary school.

99 Part 154 services for pupils with limited English proficiency. Subpart 154-1services for pupils with limited English proficiency for programs operated prior to the 2015-2016 school year

100 Several examples are provided on the official website of The Bilingual Revolution

101 Head Start is a program of the United States Department of Health and Human Services that provides comprehensive early childhood education, health, nutrition, and parent involvement services to low-income children and their families.

Notes to Chapter 12

102 For more information on this topic, read François Grosjean, Bilingual: Life and Reality.

103 You can watch this interview online: Life as Bilingual: A Conversation with Francois Grosjean by Fabrice Jaumont.

104 For more on this topic, read François Grosjean, Bilingual: Life and Reality.

105 For more information on this topic, read Daniel Goleman, The Brain and Emotional Intelligence: New Insights

106 On this topic, read Kenneth Robinson, Creative schools: The grassroots revolution that's transforming education.

107 On this topic, several studies are referenced in the bibliography section of the book, in particular Leikin (2012); Lauchlan, Parisi, & Fadda (2013); Ricciardelli (1992).

108 The concept of metalinguistic awareness refers to the ability to objectify language as a process as well as an object made by human beings. It is helpful to explaining the execution and transfer of linguistic knowledge across languages (e.g. code switching as well as translation among bilinguals).

109 For further reading on the matter, Wayne Thomas, Virginia Collier, Colin Baker, Margarita Espino Calderón and Liliana Minaya-Rowe, to name but a few, have done an excellent job of demonstrating the effectiveness of dual-language education. Their studies are listed in the bibliography section of the book.

110 For more on this topic, read Wayne Thomas & Virginia Collier, The Astounding Effectiveness of Dual-Language Education for All.

111 The American Council on the Teaching of Foreign Languages provides a list of studies about the benefits of language learning.

112 For more on this topic, read Wayne Thomas & Virginia Collier, The Astounding Effectiveness of Dual-Language Education for All.

113 On this topic, several studies conducted by Ana Ines Ansaldo and Landa Ghazi-Saidi are referenced in the bibliography section of the book

114 See, for instance, the studies of Nicoladis and Genesee (1998); Cameau, Genessee, and Lapaquette (2003) which are referenced in the bibliography.

115 See for instance Greene (1998), Thomas & Collier (2004), ou Willig (1985).

116 For more information on this topic, read Ofelia Garcia, Bilingual Education in the 21st Century: A Global Perspective.

Notes to Chapter 13

117 Visit the Center for Applied Linguistics website for more information

118 U.S. Department of Education's Office of English Language Acquisition. Dual-Language Education Programs: Current State Policies and Practices.

119 In 1974, the ASPIRA Consent Decree between the New York City Board of Education and ASPIRA of New York assured that English Language Leaners students would be provided Bilingual Education. As such, English Language Leaners must be provided with equal access to all school programs and services offered to non-English Language Leaners, including access to programs required for graduation. For more information on this topic, read De Jesús & Pérez. From Community Control to Consent Decree: Puerto Ricans organizing for education and language rights in 1960s and 1970s New York City. Read also Reyes, Luis The Aspira Consent Decree. A Thirtieth-Anniversary Retrospective of Bilingual Education in New York City. Harvard Educational Review Fall 2006 Issue

120 United States Supreme Court Case No. 72-6520

121 For more information on this topic, read Cathleen Jo Faruque, Migration of the Hmong to the Midwestern United States.

122 Minnesota is also among the states that see fostering diversity and supporting non-native English speakers as an asset and, as a result, the state has actively expanded bilingual programs for students and provided relevant resources to bilingual classroom teachers.

123 On this topic, read Kathleen Stein-Smith, The U.S. Foreign Language Deficit. Strategies for Maintaining a Competitive Edge in a Globalized World.

124 "The FBI did not dedicate sufficient resources to the surveillance and translation need of counterterrorism agents. It lacked sufficient translators proficient in Arabic and other key languages, resulting in a significant backlog of untranslated intercepts." Excerpted from page 77 of The 9/11 Commission Report – National Commission on Terrorist Attack upon the United States. July 22, 2004.

125 For more on this topic, read James Crawford. Bilingual Education: History, Politics, Theory and Practice. Trenton, NJ: Crane Publishing

Company.

126 For more on this topic, visit the ACLU American Civil Liberties Union Home Page. "English Only."

127 For more information on this topic, visit CAL's searchable databases and directories on foreign language immersion programs in schools, heritage language programs, and two-way immersion programs in the U.S.

128 David McKay Wilson, Dual-Language Programs on the Rise. "Enrichment" model puts content learning front and center for ELL students.

129 Utah Senate. International Education Initiatives – Critical Languages (Senate Bill 41)

Bibliography

References and Works Cited in the Foreword Bilingual Education: Making a U-Turn with Parents and Communities by Ofelia Garcia

Castellanos, D. L. (1983). *The Best of two worlds: Bilingual-bicultural education in the U.S.* Trenton, New Jersey: New Jersey State Dept. of Education.

Crawford, J. (2004). *Educating English learners: Language diversity in the classroom, Fifth Edition* (5th edition). Los Angeles, CA: Bilingual Education Services, Inc.

Crawford, J. (2004). *Educating English learners. Language diversity in the classroom, 5th ed. (formerly Bilingual education: History, politics, theory and practice).* Los Angeles, CA: Bilingual Educational Services.

Del Valle, S. (1998). Bilingual Education for Puerto Ricans in New York City: From Hope to Compromise. *Harvard Educational Review, 68*(2), 193–217.

Del Valle, S. (2003). *Language rights and the law in the United States.* Clevedon, UK: Multilingual Matters.

Epstein, N. (1977). *Language, Ethnicity and the Schools: Policy alternatives for bilingual-bicultural education.* Washington, D.C.: Institute for Educational Leadership.

Flores, N. (2016). A tale of two visions: Hegemonic whiteness and bilingual education. *Educational Policy, 30,* 13–38.

Flores, N. & García, O. (forthcoming). A critical review of bilingual education in the United States: From Basements and pride to boutiques and profit. *Annual Review of Applied Linguistics.*

García, O. (2011). *Bilingual education in the 21st century: A Global perspective.* Malden, MA: John Wiley & Sons.

García, O., & Fishman, J.A. (Eds.). (2001). *The Multilingual Apple. Languages in New York City* (2nd ed.). Berlin, Germany: Mouton de

Gruyter.

García, O., & Li Wei. (2014). *Translanguaging: Language, bilingualism and education*. London, United Kingdom: Palgrave Macmillan Pivot.

Lindholm-Leary, K. J. (2001). *Dual-language education*. Clevedon, UK: Multilingual Matters.

Menken, K., & Solorza, C. (2014). No Child Left Bilingual Accountability and the Elimination of Bilingual Education Programs in New York City Schools. *Educational Policy, 28*(1), 96–125.

Otheguy, R., García, O., & Reid, W. (2015). Clarifying translanguaging and deconstructing named languages: A perspective from linguistics. *Applied Linguistics Review, 6*(3), 281–307. http://doi.org/10.1515/applirev-2015-0014

Valdés, G. (1997). Dual-language immersion programs: A cautionary note concerning the education of language-minority students. Harvard Educational Review, 67, 391-429.

References and Works Cited in
The Bilingual Education: The Future of Education is in Two Languages by Fabrice Jaumont

American Council on the Teaching of Foreign Languages. What the Research Shows. Studies supporting language acquisition. Retrieved on July 11, 2017.

American Civil Liberties Union (ACLU). ACLU Backgrounder on English Only Policies in Congress. Retrieved on August 21, 2017.

Ansaldo, A.I., & Ghazi Saidi, L. (2014) Aphasia therapy in the age of globalization: Cross-linguistic therapy effects in bilingual aphasia. *Behavioural Neurology*. Volume 2014 (March)

Ansaldo, A.I. Ghazi-Saidi, L & Adrover-Roig, D. (2015) Interference Control in Elderly Bilinguals: Appearances can be misleading. *Journal of Clinical and Experimental Neuropsychology*. Volume 37, issue 5. February 2015. (pp. 455-470)

Ascenzi-Moreno, L. and Flores, N. A case study of bilingual policy and practices at the Cypress Hills Community School. In O. Garcia, B. Otcu & Z. Zakharia (Eds.), *Bilingual Community Education and*

Multilingualism: Beyond Heritage Languages in a Global City (pp. 219-231). Bristol, UK: Multilingual Matters.

Aspira v. Board of Education of City of New York. 394 F. Supp. 1161 (1975).

August, D. and Hakuta, K. (Eds,) (1997) *Improving Schooling for Language-Minority Children.* Washington, DC: National Academy Press.

Ball, J. (2010, February). *Educational equity for children from diverse language backgrounds: Mother tongue-based bilingual or multilingual education in the early years.* Presentation to UNESCO International Symposium: Translation and Cultural Mediation, Paris, France.

Baker, C. (2014). *A parents' and teachers' guide to bilingualism.* Bristol, U.K. Multilingual Matters.

Baker, C. (2001). *Foundations of bilingual education and bilingualism* (3rd ed.). Clevedon, UK: Multilingual Matters.

Barac, R., Bialystok, E., Castro, D. C., & Sanchez, M. (2014). The cognitive development of young dual-language learners: A critical review. *Early Childhood Research Quarterly, 29*(4), 699–714.

Barrière, I., & Monéreau-Merry, M.M. (2012). Trilingualism of the Haitian Diaspora in NYC: Current and Future Challenges. In O. Garcia, B. Otcu & Z. Zakharia (Eds.), Bilingual Community Education and Multilingualism: Beyond Heritage Languages in a Global City (pp. 247-258). Bristol, UK: Multilingual Matters.

Barrière, I. (2010). The vitality of Yiddish among Hasidic infants and toddlers in a low SES preschool in Brooklyn. In W. Moskovich (Ed.), Yiddish - A Jewish National Language at 100 (pp. 170 – 196). Jerusalem-Kyiv: Hebrew University of Jerusalem.

Brisk, M., & Proctor, P. (2012). *Challenges and supports for English language learners in bilingual programs.* Paper presented at the Understanding Language Conference, Stanford University, Stanford, CA.

Brisk, M. E. (1998) *Bilingual Education: From Compensatory to Quality Schooling.* Mahwah, NJ: Lawrence Erlbaum Associates.

Calderón, M. E., & Minaya-Rowe, L. (2003). *Designing and implementing two-way bilingual programs.* Thousand Oaks, CA: Corwin Press.

Canadian Parents for French. (2012). *The State of French-Second-Language Education in Canada 2012: Academically Challenged Students and FSL Programs.*

Cameau, L., Genesee, F., and Lapaquette, L. (2003). The modelling hypothesis and child bilingual code-mixing. *International Journal of Bilingualism*, 7.2:113-128

Castellón, M., Cheuk, T., Greene, R., Mercado-Garcia, D., Santos, M., Skarin, R. & Zerkel, L. (2015). *Schools to Learn from: How Six High Schools Graduate English Language Learners College and Career Ready*. Prepared for Carnegie Corporation of New York. Stanford Graduate School of Education. *Castaneda v. Pickard*. 648 F.2d 989 (1981).

Center for Applied Linguistics. Two-Way Immersion Outreach Project.

Center for Applied Linguistics. Databases and directories.

Christian, D. (1996). Two-way immersion education: Students learning through two languages. *The Modern Language Journal, 80*(1), 66–76.

Christian, D. (2011). Dual-language education. In E. Hinkel (Ed.), *Handbook of research in second language teaching and learning, volume II* (pp. 3–20). New York, NY: Routledge.

Cloud, N., Genesee, F., & Hamayan, E. (2000). *Dual-Language Instruction: A Handbook for Enriched Education*. Boston, MA: Heinle & Heinle, Thomson Learning, Inc.

Combs, M., Evans, C., Fletcher, T., Parra, E., & Jiménez, A. (2005). Bilingualism for the children: Implementing a dual-language program in an English-only state. *Educational Policy, 19*(5), 701–728.

Crawford, J. (2004). *Educating English learners. Language diversity in the classroom* (Fifth Ed.). Los Angeles, CA: Bilingual Educational Services, Inc.

Crawford, J. (1999). *Bilingual Education: History, Politics, Theory and Practice*. Trenton, NJ: Crane Publishing Company.

Cummins, J., & Swain, M. (1986). *Bilingualism in education: Aspects of theory, research and practice*. London: Longman

De Jesús, A. & Pérez, M. (2009). From Community Control to Consent Decree: Puerto Ricans organizing for education and language rights in 1960s and 1970s New York City. *CENTRO Journal* 7 Volume xx1 Number 2 fall 2009

de Jong, E. (2004). L2 proficiency development in a two-way and a developmental bilingual program. *NABE Journal of Research and Practice*, 2(1), 77–108.

de Jong, E. J. (2014). Program design and two-way immersion programs. *Journal of Immersion and Content-Based Language Education, 2*(2), 241–256.

de Jong, E. J., & Bearse, C. I. (2014). Dual-language programs as a strand within a secondary school: Dilemmas of school organization and the TWI mission. *International Journal of Bilingual Education and Bilingualism, 17*(1), 15–31.

de Jong, E. J., & Howard, E. (2009). Integration in two-way immersion education: Equalising linguistic benefits for all students. *International Journal of Bilingual Education and Bilingualism, 12*(1), 81–99.

Dorner, L. (2010). Contested communities in a debate over dual-language education: The import of "public" values on public policies. *Educational Policy, 25*(4), 577–613.

Elliott, A. Muslim educator's dream branded a threat in the U.S. *New York Times*. April 28, 2008.

Espinosa, L. (2013). *Early education for dual-language learners: Promoting school readiness and early school success.* Washington, DC: Migration Policy Institute.

Faruque, Cathleen Jo. *Migration of the Hmong to the Midwestern United States.* Lanham, NY: University Press of America, Inc., 2002.

Fishman. J. (editor). (1999). *Handbook of language and ethnic identity.* Oxford, U.K.: Oxford University Press.

Fishman, J. (1976). *Bilingual education: An international sociological perspective.* Rowley, MA: Newbury House.

Flores v. Arizona. 160 F. Supp. 2d 1043 (D. Ariz. 2000).

Flores, N., & Rosa, J. (2015). Undoing appropriateness: Raciolinguistic ideologies and language diversity in education. *Harvard Educational Review*, 85, 149–171.

Flores, N., & Baetens Beardsmore, H. (2015). Programs and structures in bilingual and multilingual education. In W. Wright, S. Boun, & O.García (Eds.), *Handbook of bilingual and multilingual education* (pp. 205–222). Oxford, UK: Wiley-Blackwell.

Flores, N. (2014). Creating republican machines: Language governmentality in the United States. *Linguistics and Education*, 25(1), 1–11.

Flores, N. (2013). Silencing the subaltern: Nation-state/colonial governmentality and bilingual education in the United States. *Critical Inquiry in Language Studies*, 10(4), 263–287.

Fortune. T.& Tedick, D. (Eds.). (2008) *Pathways to multilingualism: Evolving perspectives on immersion education.* Clevedon, England: Multilingual Matters.

Freeman, R. D. (1998). *Bilingual education and social change.* Clevedon, UK: Multilingual Matters.

Galush, William J. (2006). For More Than Bread: Community and Identity in American Polonia, 1880–1940. East European Monographs. New York: Columbia University Press

Garcia, E. E. (2005). *Teaching and learning in two languages: bilingualism & schooling in the United States* (Multicultural Education)

García, O. (2009). *Bilingual education in the 21ˢᵗ century: A global perspective.* Oxford, UK: Wiley-Blackwell.

Garcia, O., and Kleifgen, J.A. (2010) *Educating Emergent Bilinguals: Policies, Programs, and Practices for English Language Learners.* New York: Teachers College Press.

García O., Zakharia Z., and Otcu, B., (editors). (2002). *Bilingual community education and multilingualism. beyond heritage languages in a global city*, (Bristol, U.K.: Multilingual Matters)

García, O., Johnson, S.I., Seltzer, K (2016). *The translanguaging classroom: leveraging student bilingualism for learning.* Philadelphia, Pennsylvania: Caslon.

Genesee, F., Lindholm-Leary, K., Saunders, W., & Christian, D. (Eds.) (2006). Educating English language learners: A synthesis of research evidence. New York: Cambridge University Press.

Ghazi Saidi L., Perlbarg V., Marrelec G., Pélégrini-Issac M., Benali H. & Ansaldo AI. (2013) Functional connectivity changes in second language vocabulary learning. Brain Language, Jan; 124 (1):56-65.

Ghazi-Saidi, L. & Ansaldo, A. I. (2015) Can a Second Language Help You in More Ways Than One? Commentary article. AIMS Neuroscience, 2(1):52-5

Ghazi Saidi, L., Dash, T. & Ansaldo, A. I. (In Press), How Native-Like Can You Possibly Get: fMRI Evidence in a pair of Linguistically close

Languages, Special Issue: Language beyond words: the neuroscience of accent, Frontiers in Neuroscience, 9.

Goldenberg, C. (2006). Improving Achievement for English Learners: Conclusions from Two Research Reviews. *Education Week. July 25, 2006.*

Goleman, D. (2011). *The Brain and Emotional Intelligence: New Insights.* Florence, MA. More than Sound.

Gómez, D. S. (2013). *Bridging the opportunity gap through dual-language education.* Unpublished manuscript, California State University, Stanislaus.

Gómez, L., Freeman, D., & Freeman, Y. (2005). Dual-language education: A promising 50-50 model. *Bilingual Research Journal, 29*(1), 145–164.

Gongolski, C. & Cesarczyk, M. Two languages, one home. *Greenpoint News.* September 16, 2015.

Greene, J. (1998) A Meta-Analysis of the Effectiveness of Bilingual Education.

Grosjean, F. (2010) *Bilingual: Life and reality.* Cambridge, MA. Harvard University Press.

Grosjean, F. (1982). *Life with two languages: An introduction to bilingualism.* Cambridge, MA. Harvard University Press.

Hakuta, K. (1986). Mirror of language: The debate on bilingualism. NY: Basic Books.

Harris, E. "New York City Education Department to Add or Expand 40 Dual-Language Programs." *New York Times.* January 14, 2015.

Hélot, C. & Erfurt, E. (2016) *L'éducation bilingue en France : politiques linguistiques, modèles et pratiques.* Rennes, Presses Universitaires de Rennes.

Howard, E. R., & Christian, D. (2002). *Two-way immersion 101: Designing and implementing a two-way immersion education program at the elementary level.* Santa Cruz, CA: Center for Research on Education, Diversity, and Excellence, University of California-Santa Cruz.

Howard, E. R., Sugarman, J., Christian, D., Lindholm-Leary, K., & Rogers, D. (2007). *Guiding Principles for Dual-Language Education.* Second Edition Center for Applied Linguistics.

Howard, E., Sugarman, J., & Coburn, C. (2006). *Adapting the Sheltered Instruction Observation Protocol (SIOP) for two-way immersion education: An introduction to the TWIOP.* Washington DC: Center for Applied Linguistics.

Jaumont, F.; Ross, J.; Schulz, J.; Ducrey, L.; Dunn, J. (2017) "Sustainability of French Heritage Language Education in the United States" in Peter P. Trifonas and Thermistoklis Aravossitas (editors) *International Handbook on Research and Practice in Heritage Language Education.* New York, NY: Springer.

Jaumont, F., Le Devedec, B. & Ross J. (2016). "Institutionalization of French Heritage Language Education in U.S. School Systems: The French Heritage Language Program" in Olga Kagan, Maria Carreira, Claire Chik (editors). *Handbook on Heritage Language Education: From Innovation to Program Building.* Oxford, U.K.: Routledge.

Jaumont, F., Cogard, K. (2016). *Trends and Supports on French Immersion and Bilingual Education in 2015.* A Report of the Cultural Services of the French Embassy to the United States.

Jaumont, F. Life as Bilingual: A Conversation with Francois Grosjean. (2015).

Jaumont, F. & Ross, J. (2014). "French Heritage Language Communities in the United States" in Terrence Wiley, Joy Peyton, Donna Christian, Sarah Catherine Moore, Na Liu. (editors). *Handbook of Heritage and Community Languages in the United States: Research, Educational Practice, and Policy.* Oxford, U.K.: Routledge

Jaumont, F. & Ross, J. (2012). Building Bilingual Communities: New York's French Bilingual Revolution" in Ofelia García, Zeena Zakharia, and Bahar Otcu, (editors). *Bilingual Community Education and Multilingualism. Beyond Heritage Languages in a Global City* (pp.232-246). Bristol, U.K.: Multilingual Matters.

Jaumont, F. & Ross, J. (2013). French Heritage Language Vitality in the United States." *Heritage Language Journal.* Volume 9. Number 3.

Jaumont, F. (2012). The French Bilingual Revolution. *Language Magazine.* The Journal of Communication & Education. June 1st 2012.

Joint National Committee for Languages - National Council for Languages and International Studies.

Kagan, O., Carreira, M., Chik, C. (editors). (2016). *Handbook on Heritage Language Education: From Innovation to Program Building.* (Oxford, U.K.: Routledge, in press).

Kay, K. (2010). 21st century skills: Why they matter, what they are, and how we get there. In J. Bellanca & R. Brandt (Eds.), *21st century skills: Rethinking how students learn* (pp. xiii– xxxi). Bloomington, IN: Solution Tree Press.

Kayyali, R. The people perceived as a threat to security: Arab Americans since September 11. *Migration Policy.* July 1, 2006.

Kelleher, A. (2010). Who is a heritage language learner? *Heritage Briefs.* Washington, DC: Center for Applied Linguistics.

Keyes v. School Dist. No. 1, Denver, Colorado. 413 U.S. 189 (1973)

Kleyn, T., & Vayshenker, B. Russian Bilingual Education across Public, Private and Community Spheres. In O. Garcia, B. Otcu & Z. Zakharia (Eds.), Bilingual Community Education and Multilingualism: Beyond Heritage Languages in a Global City (pp. 259-271). Bristol, UK: Multilingual Matters.

Kleyn, T., & Reyes, S. (2011). Nobody said it would be easy: Ethnolinguistic group challenges to bilingual and multicultural education in New York City. *International Journal of Bilingual Education and Bilingualism*, 14(2), 207-224

Kleyn, T. (2008). Speaking in colors: A window into uncomfortable conversations about race and ethnicity in U.S. bilingual classrooms. GiST: The Colombian Journal of Bilingual Education, 2: 13-23.

Lau v. Nichols, 414 U.S. 563 (1974).

Lauchlan, F; Parisi, M.; Fadda, R. (2013). Bilingualism in Sardinia and Scotland: Exploring the cognitive benefits of speaking a 'minority' language International *Journal of Bilingualism* February 2013 17: 43-56, first published on April 16, 2012

Leikin, M. (2012) The effect of bilingualism on creativity: Developmental and educational perspectives. *International Journal of Bilingualism* August 2013 17: 431-447, first published on March 28, 2012

Liebtag, E., & Haugen, C. (2015, April 29). *Shortage of dual-language teachers: Filling the gap.*

Lindholm-Leary, K.J. (1990). Bilingual Immersion Education: Criteria for Program Development. Bilingual Education: Issues and Strategies, Padilla, A.M, Fairchild, H.H, & Valadez, C.M. (Eds.).

Lindholm-Leary, K. J. (2001). Dual-language education. Clevedon, UK: Multilingual Matters.

Lindholm-Leary, K.J. (2000). Biliteracy for a Global Society: An Idea Book on Dual-Language Education. Washington, DC: The George Washington University.

Lindholm-Leary, K. J. (2003). Dual-language achievement, proficiency, and attitudes among current high school graduates of two-way programs. *NABE Journal, 26,* 20–25.

Lindholm-Leary, K. (2012). Success and challenges in dual-language education. *Theory Into Practice, Special Issue: Rethinking Language Teaching and Learning in Multilingual Classrooms, 51*(4), 256–262.

Lindholm-Leary, K., & Genesee, F. (2014). Student outcomes in one-way, two-way, and indigenous language immersion education. *Journal of Immersion and Content-Based Language Education, 2*(2), 165–180.

Lopez Estrada, V., Gómez, L., & Ruiz-Escalante, J. (2009). Let's make dual-language the norm. *Educational Leadership, 66*(7), 54–58.

McKay Wilson, D. (2011). Dual-language programs on the rise. "Enrichment" model puts content learning front and center for ELL students. *Harvard Education Letter.* Volume 27, Number 2 March/April 2011

Marian, V., Shook, A., & Schroeder, S. R. (2013). Bilingual two-way immersion programs benefit academic achievement. *Bilingual Research Journal, 36,* 167–186.

McCabe, A., et al. (2013). Multilingual children: Beyond myths and toward best practices. *Social Policy Report, 27*(4).

Menken, K., & Garcia, O. (Eds.). (2010). *Negotiating language policies in schools: Educators as policymakers.* New York, NY: Routledge.

Menken, K., & Solorza, C. (2014). No child left bilingual: Accountability and the elimination of bilingual education programs in New York City schools. *Educational Policy, 28*(1), 96– 125.

Meyer v. Nebraska. 262 U.S. 390 (1923).

Millard, M. (2015). *State funding mechanisms for English language learners.* Denver, CO: Education Commission of the States.

Mitchell, C. (2015, June 10). New York expanding dual-language to help its English learners. *Education Week, 34*(34), 7.

Montague, N. S. (2005). Essential beginnings for dual-language programs. *The TABE Journal, 8,* 18–25.

Montone, C. L., & Loeb, M. I. (2000). *Implementing two-way immersion programs in secondary schools.* Santa Cruz, CA: Center for Research on Education, Diversity & Excellence.

National Commission on Terrorist Attack upon the United States. July 22, 2004. Government Printing Office.

National Standards Collaborative Board. (2015). *World-Readiness Standards for Learning Languages* (4th ed.). Alexandria, VA: Author.

National Standards in Foreign Language Education Project. (2006). *Standards for foreign language learning in the 21st century.* Lawrence, KS: Allen Press, Inc

Nevel, D. The Slow Death of Khalil Gibran International Academy. *Chalkbeat.* April 20, 2011.

New Visions for Public Schools. Center for School Success. (2001). Best Practices Series. Dual-Language Instruction.

New York City Department of Education (2015). Chancellor Fariña names 15 schools Model Dual-Language Programs. Press Release. December 03, 2015.

New York City Department of Education, Office of School Quality, Division of Teaching and Learning. (2015). Quality review report – High School for Dual Language and Asian Studies.

New York State Department of Education. (2014). Part 154 services for pupils with limited English proficiency. Subpart 154-1services for pupils with limited English proficiency for programs operated prior to the 2015-2016 school year.

Nicoladis, E, and Genesee, F. (1998). Parental discourse and code-mixing in bilingual children. *International Journal of Bilingualism* 2.1:422 -432.

Ó'Murchú, H. (2001) *The Irish language in education in the Republic of Ireland.* European Research Centre on Multilingualism and Language Learning.

Otcu, B. (2010). *Language Maintenance and cultural identity formation.* Saarbrucken: VDM Verlag Dr. Muller.

Otcu, B. (2010). Heritage language maintenance and cultural identity formation: The case of a Turkish Saturday school in New York City. *Heritage Language Journal,* 7(2) Fall, 2010.

Paciotto, C., & Delany-Barmann, G. (2011). Planning micro-level language education reform in new diaspora sites: Two-way immersion education in the rural Midwest. *Language Policy, 10*(3), 221–243.

Palmer, D. (2007). A dual immersion strand programme in California: Carrying out the promise of dual-language education in an English-dominant context. *International Journal of Bilingual Education and Bilingualism, 10*(6), 752–768.

Palmer, D. (2010). Race, power, and equity in a multiethnic urban elementary school with a dual-language "strand" program. *Anthropology & Education Quarterly, 41*(1), 94–114.

Parkes, J., & Ruth, T. (with Angberg-Espinoza, A., & de Jong, E.). (2009). *Urgent research questions and issues in dual-language education.* Albuquerque, NM: Dual-Language Education of New Mexico.

Parkes, J., & Ruth, T. (2011). How satisfied are parents of students in dual-language education programs? 'Me parece maravillosa la gran oportunidad que le están dando a estos niños.' *International Journal of Bilingual Education and Bilingualism, 14*(6), 701–718.

Phillips, J. K., & Abbott, M. (2011). *A decade of foreign language standards: Impact, influence, and future directions.* Alexandria, VA: American Council on the Teaching of Foreign Languages.

Porras, D. A., Ee, J., & Gandara, P. C. (2014). Employer preferences: Do bilingual applicants and employees experience an advantage? In R. M. Callahan & P. C. Gándara (Eds.), *The bilingual advantage: Language, literacy, and the labor market* (pp. 234–257). Clevedon, UK: Multilingual Matters.

Porter, R. P. *Forked Tongue: The Politics of Bilingual Education.* New Brunswick, NJ: Transaction Publishers, 1996.

Ramirez, J. D., Yuen, S. D., Ramey, D. R., & Pasta, D. J. (1991). *Executive Summary. Final Report: Longitudinal Study of Structured English Immersion Strategy, Early-Exit and Late-Exit Transitional Bilingual Education Programs for Language Minority Children.* San Mateo, CA: Aguirre International.

Reyes, L. The *Aspira Consent Decree. A Thirtieth-Anniversary Retrospective* of Bilingual Education in New York City. Harvard Educational Review Fall 2006 Issue

Rhodes, N. C., & Pufahl, I. (2010). *Foreign language teaching in US Schools: Results of a national survey.* Washington, DC: Center for Applied Linguistics.

Ricciardelli, L. A. (1992), Creativity and Bilingualism. The Journal of Creative Behavior, 26: 242–254

Robinson, K. (2015). Creative schools: The grassroots revolution that's transforming education. New York, NY: Viking.

Rosenback, R. (2014). Bringing Up a Bilingual Child. Croydon, U.K. Filament Publishing.

Rossell, C. H. and K. Baker. "The Educational Effectiveness of Bilingual Education." *Research in the Teaching of English* 30, no. 1 (February 1996): 7-74.

Sandhofer, C., & Uchikoshi, Y. (2013). Cognitive consequences of dual-language learning: Cognitive function, language and literacy, science and mathematics, and social-emotional development. In F. Ong & J. McLean (Eds.), *California's best practices for young dual-language learners: Research overview papers* (pp. 51–89). Sacramento, CA: California Department of Education.

Sandy-Sanchez, D. (2008). Secondary dual-language guiding principles: A review of the process. *Soleado,* 8.

Santos, M., Darling-Hammond, L., & Cheuk, T. (2012). *Teacher development appropriate to support ELLs.* Stanford, CA: Understanding Language.

Saunders, W., & O'Brien, G. (2006). Oral language. In F. Genesee, K. Lindholm-Leary, W. Saunders, & D. Christian (Eds.), *Educating English language learners: A synthesis of research evidence* (pp. 14–63). New York, NY: Cambridge University Press.

Scanlan, M., & Palmer, D. (2009). Race, power, and (in) equity within two-way immersion settings. *The Urban Review, 41*(5), 391–415.

Semple, K. A Big Advocate of French in New York's Schools: France. *New York Times.* January 30, 2014.

Serna v. Portales Municipal Schools. 351 F. Supp. 1279 (1972)

Silberstein, R. New York's first Italian dual-language preschool coming to Bensonhurst. January 30, 2015. *Bensonhurst Bean.*

Soltero, S. W. (2016). *Dual-language education: Program design and implementation.* Portsmouth, NH: Heinemann.

Stein-Smith, K. (2016). The U.S. Foreign Language Deficit. Strategies for Maintaining a Competitive Edge in a Globalized World. New York, NY: Palgrave-Macmillan.

Stein-Smith, K. (2013). The U.S. Foreign Language Deficit and Our Economic and National Security: A Bibliographic Essay on the U.S. Language Paradox. Edwin Mellen Press, NY.

Tedick, D. J., & Bjorklund, S. (Eds.). (2014). Language immersion education: A research agenda for 2015 and beyond. *Journal of Immersion and Content-Based Language Education, 2, 2.*

The National Center for Research on Cultural Diversity and Second Language Learning (1996). *Learning Together: Two-Way Bilingual Immersion Programs.* Video. Produced by Jon Silver.

Thomas, W. P., & Collier, V. P. The Astounding Effectiveness of Dual-Language Education for All. *NABE Journal of Research and Practice,* 2:1. Winter 2004.

Thomas, W. P., & Collier, V. P. (1997/1998). Two languages are better than one. Educational Leadership, 55(4), 23–26.

Thomas, W. P., & Collier, V. P. (1999). Accelerated schooling for English-language learners. Educational Leadership, 56(7), 46–49.

Thomas, W. P., & Collier, V. P. (2002). A national study of school effectiveness for language minority students' long-term academic achievement. Santa Cruz, CA: Center for Research on Education, Diversity, and Excellence, University of California-Santa Cruz.

Thomas, W. P., & Collier, V. P. (1998). *Language Minority Student Achievement and Program Effectiveness: Research Summary of Ongoing Study.* George Mason University.

Tochon, F. V. (2009). The key to global understanding: World Languages Education—Why schools need to adapt. *Review of Educational Research,* 79(2), 650–681.

Torres-Guzmán, M., Kleyn, T., Morales-Rodríguez, S., & Han, A. (2005). Self-designated dual-language programs: Is there a gap between labeling and implementation? *Bilingual Research Journal*, *29*(2), 453–474.

U.S. Department of Education, Office of English Language Acquisition (2015). Dual-Language Education Programs: Current State Policies and Practices, Washington, D.C.

U.S. Department of Education, Office for Civil Rights, and U.S. Department of Justice, Civil Rights Division. (2015). *Dear colleague letter, English learner students and limited English proficient parents.* Washington, DC: Author.

U.S. News Report High School Rankings: High School for Dual Language and Asian Studies.

Utah Senate (2008). International Education Initiatives – Critical Languages (Senate Bill 41)

Wall, P. City to add dozens of dual-language programs as they grow in popularity. *Chalkbeat*. April 4, 2016.

Warhol, L., & Mayer, A. (2012). Misinterpreting school reform: The dissolution of a dual-immersion bilingual program in an urban New England elementary school. *Bilingual Research Journal*, *35*(2), 145–163.

Wiley, T., Peyton, J., Christian, D., Moore, S.C., Liu. **N.** (editors). (2014). Handbook of Heritage and Community Languages in the United States: Research, Educational Practice, and Policy. (Oxford, U.K.: Routledge).

Willig, A. (1985). A meta-analysis of selected studies on the effectiveness of bilingual education. Review of Educational Research, 55, 269-317.

Wright, W. (2015). *Foundations for Teaching English Language Learners: Research, Theory, Policy, and Practice.* Philadelphia, PA: Caslon.

Yang Su, E. (2012). *Dual-language lessons growing in popularity.* Emeryville, CA: California Watch.

Zakharia, Z. (2016) Language, conflict, and migration: Situating Arabic bilingual community education in the United States. *International Journal of the Sociology of Language.* 2016; 237: 139–160.

Zakharia, Z. & Menchaca Bishop, L. (2013). Towards positive peace through bilingual community education: Language efforts of Arabic-speaking communities in New York. In Ofelia García, Zeena Zakharia & Bahar Otcu (eds.), *Bilingual community education and multilingualism: Beyond heritage languages in a global city*, 169–189. Bristol: Multilingual Matters.

Zanoni, C. Principal Miriam Pedraja teaches Uptown children two languages at a time. *DNAInfo*. April 16, 2012.

Zeigler, K & Camarota, S. One in Five U.S. Residents Speaks Foreign Language at Home. October 2015. Center for Immigration Studies.

Zimmer, A. How Schools' French Dual-Language Programs Are Changing NYC Neighborhoods. *DNAInfo*. May 26, 2015.

Index

P.S. 20, 51
P.S. 200, 43, 44, 141
P.S. 25, 75
P.S. 34, 65, 66, 68, 69, 142
P.S. 84, 52, 75
P.S./I.S. 30, 60, 62, 142
P.S.58, 49, 139
parents, 5, i, ii, 1, 8, 9, 1, 2, 3, 5,
  6, 7, 8, 9, 10, 11, 12, 13, 14,
  17, 18, 19, 20, 21, 22, 23, 24,
  25, 26, 27, 28, 29, 30, 31, 32,
  33, 36, 37, 38, 39, 41, 42, 43,
  44, 46, 50, 51, 52, 53, 54, 55,
  59, 60, 61, 62, 63, 65, 66, 67,
  68, 69, 74, 75, 76, 77, 78,
  79,81, 83, 89, 90, 91, 94, 95,
  97, 99, 100, 101, 103, 107,
  119, 120, 121, 122, 125, 126,
  127, 131, 134, 136, 144, 151,
  160, 163
Park Slope, 33, 53
Pennsylvania, 2, 154
policy, 3, 61, 75, 78, 106, 150
Polish, 2, 9, 4, 65, 66, 67, 68, 69,
  70, 91, 119
Portuguese, 112, 116
pre-Kindergarten, 23
Principal, 8, 9, 11, 12, 23, 27, 28,
  44, 49, 50, 52, 57, 60, 65, 68,
  75, 76, 77, 78, 83, 85, 94, 96,
  97, 98, 99, 100, 132, 133, 135,
  136
Public, 4, 22, 50, 55, 77, 78, 141,
  157, 159
public school, ii, 3, 8, 9, 17, 20,
  22, 29, 33, 37, 45, 50, 53, 54,
  57, 58, 62, 75, 89, 97, 113,
  114, 125
public schools, i, ii, 1, 2, 3, 5, 7,
  2, 4, 5, 6, 17, 18, 21, 24, 28,
  29, 30, 35, 50, 53, 54, 55, 56,
  60, 69, 76, 77, 89, 94, 113,
  117, 119, 121
Qatar Foundation International,
  60, 142

Quebec Government
  Delegation, 55
Queens, 34, 38, 42, 51, 55, 76,
  79
revolution, 5, iii, 1, 8, 9, 4, 15,
  50, 70, 78, 121, 141, 145, 161
roadmap, 5, ii, 2, 9, 3, 18, 21, 89,
  90, 100, 122, 125, 144
Ronald Reagan, 5
Roosevelt, 4
Russia, 41, 45
Russian, ii, 2, 9, 4, 24, 27, 41,
  42, 43, 44, 45, 46, 61, 97, 112,
  116, 119, 143, 144, 157
segregated, 3, 6, 22, 78
Senate, 55, 116, 147, 163
*Société des Professeurs de Français et
  Francophones d'Amérique*, 54,
  141
South Bronx, 51
Spanish, 2, 3, 6, 7, 9, 4, 8, 11,
  12, 42, 43, 44, 52, 54, 73, 74,
  75, 76, 77, 78, 79, 81, 85, 90,
  108, 112, 114, 116, 119
state, 1, 3, 20, 41, 52, 82, 93,
  100, 112, 121, 129, 136, 139,
  146, 152, 154
Supreme Court, 4, 114, 146
teachers, 5, i, 1, 8, 9, 3, 8, 9, 13,
  14, 18, 19, 21, 22, 23, 26, 28,
  38, 41, 46, 54, 65, 67, 77, 78,
  79, 85, 89, 96, 97, 98, 99, 100,
  101, 108, 121, 130, 131, 133,
  134, 136, 141, 144, 146, 151,
  157
test scores, 11, 19
testing, 18, 140
Texas, 3
third grade, 62, 78
training, 23
transitional, 5, 4, 75, 93, 105,
  111, 114, 115
translanguaging, 7, 108, 150, 154
U.S.A. *See* United States
United States, 5, i, ii, 1, 3, 4, 1,
  3, 4, 5, 6, 7, 10, 19, 20, 25, 26,

Fabrice Jaumont is the author of *Unequal Partners: American Foundations and Higher Education Development in Africa* (Palgrave-MacMillan, 2016); *The Bilingual Revolution: The Future of Education is in Two Languages* (TBR Books, 2017), which has been translated in Arabic, Chinese, French, German, Russian, and Spanish; *Partenaires inégaux. Fondations américaines et universités en Afrique* (Editions de la Maison des sciences de l'homme, 2018) ; and *Stanley Kubrick : The Odysseys* (Books We Live By, 2018).

A native of France, Fabrice Jaumont moved to the United States in 1997. He is currently a Program Director for FACE Foundation in New York, and Education Attaché for the Embassy of France to the United States. He is also a Senior Fellow at Fondation Maison des Sciences de l'Homme in Paris. Fabrice Jaumont holds a Ph.D. in Comparative and International Education from New York University.

In recognition of his various involvements in education and culture, Fabrice Jaumont was honored with several awards including the Cultural Diversity Award; the Academic Palms; and the Medal of Honor. His work received the accolades of various news media.

fabricejaumont.net

A Brooklyn-based, independent publisher with a focus on authors with revolutionary ideas for culture, education, and human development.

Fabrice Jaumont's The Bilingual Revolution is available in Arabic, English, German, French, Russian, Spanish, and soon in Chinese, Italian, Japanese, and Polish. All books are available as paperback and ebooks. The English and French versions are also available as hardcover and audiobooks.

For a listing of books published by TBR Books, or for our submission guidelines, visit our website at:

tbr-books.com